WORK-LIFE *HARMONY*

WORK-LIFE

~~BALANCE~~

HARMONY

Enjoy your life and family more because of
(not in spite of) your work.

GRANT BOTMA

WORK-LIFE HARMONY

Enjoy Your Life and Family More
Because of (Not in Spite Of) Your Work

ISBN 978-1-5445-2370-5 *Hardcover*
      978-1-5445-2368-2 *Paperback*
      978-1-5445-2369-9 *Ebook*
      978-1-5445-2371-2 *Audiobook*

This book is dedicated to my wife, Jodie, for not only putting in the time to write a chapter of this book, but for being on this journey of work-life harmony with me from day one of our marriage.

CONTENTS

INTRODUCTION

"Music is nothing else but wild sounds civilized into time and tune."

—THOMAS FULLER

Imagine attending a child's second-grade recital.

You take time off work, drive all the way across town, battle the other parents for parking, and finally find a decent seat near the stage, just before the curtains come up. Your phone is out, ready to record, and all the kids look *so cute!*

The show begins. At first, they play pretty well. For a few bars, the music sounds better than you expected. You are so proud of your child and so excited to see them up on that stage, performing their heart out.

But that magical moment doesn't last long...and the recital suddenly seems to drag on forever.

Somebody starts singing off tempo. Three or four of the instruments play the wrong notes. Then one entire section of the choir loses it completely, with everybody singing off-key. The next thing you know, everyone on stage is doing their own thing, taking the song in thirty different directions. The music teacher does her best to keep everything together, but it is impossible to balance it all. It's *chaos*.

You're still clinging to that feeling of pride and excitement to see your child perform...but if you're honest with yourself, that joy is quickly overcome by reality. This is a children's concert, and it is not amazing. Instead of enjoying the moment, you are now enduring it. You try to balance the love and pride you have for your child with your frustration at having to sit through the truly terrible music being played. You could have been working—doing something actually productive—or, heck, watching the game on TV would be better than this! *How much longer can this go on?*

You sit there with a fake smile plastered on your face, while inside your head it sounds like one of those windup monkey toys is playing the cymbals on your brain.

You can't even find the words for what you're experiencing. It isn't music—and it's certainly not harmony.

OUT OF BALANCE

The goal in music is to have harmony—and that should be your goal in life as well. Unfortunately, a lot of people are told that they should instead focus on having work-life *balance*.

"But, Grant," you may be thinking, "what's wrong with trying to have balance?"

There's nothing inherently wrong with balance, but let's take a look at what that means and what it looks like in your life.

Think about walking on a balance beam. One end of the balance beam is work and the other end is home. You walk slowly in one direction, and you can actually see the other end...but it's *so hard* to get there. You have to walk slowly and carefully. Occasionally you have to wave your arms in circles, leaning one way and then the other, trying to keep that precious balance. It's a struggle, requiring both physical and mental energy, but you finally make it to one end of the beam...only to have someone tell you that you have to turn around and go back, that you need to spend an equal amount of time at the other end of the beam.

So you have to keep walking back and forth, trying to balance. Some days that balance beam seems longer than others. Sometimes you're closer to the work end and you look back at home and see how far away it is. Other times you're on the home side and missing out on opportunities on the work side of things. Either way, you are left to balance all alone. You're lonely. And you feel like a failure because work isn't going the way you want and your home life isn't going well either. Deep down, you know this isn't how it's supposed to be. It's supposed to be different, *better*. Why can't you find your balance?

Then someone comes along and tells you the real kicker: you have to continue walking that balance beam for the rest of your life. You will continue working this hard to keep your balance *forever*, because if you stop, everything will fall apart.

Pretty grim, right?

But you're smart. You're a hard worker, and you can make things happen. You will *learn* to balance it all. Right?

A man named Suresh Joachim holds sixteen Guinness world records, including one for being the person able to balance on one foot the longest. His record? Seventy-six hours and forty minutes. I think that's pretty impressive.

But this is the *best balancer in the world*, and even he could only stay balanced for a few days.

So why is work–life balance our goal? Why do we focus on juggling work and life and everything else, when if all we're going for is balance, just like Joachim, eventually we're going to fall down?

You may be wondering what that looks like, what it *feels* like, when you try to balance but fail.

Well, mostly it feels lonely. You are doing really well at work, advancing your career and making a great income to provide for your family—yet you feel like your family doesn't appreciate you, and that hurts. You wish that the people closest to you could know just how good you are at your job, how hard you work and how much you sacrifice, as well as the true impact you make in your workplace.

Think about it: the people you care about most in the world have no idea just how good you are at doing something that helps take care of them.

And I know you have great intentions. You don't want to be awesome only at work; you want to be the best spouse and parent possible, too. You want to spend time with your partner and your kids, and you want to *focus on them*. You want to know what's happening in their lives, to hurt when they hurt and feel joy when they feel joy. You want to share with them the most important areas of your life, to be deeply connected.

But, sadly, this inability to balance only leaves you feeling more *disconnected* from your spouse and kids. You are scared that if things continue as they have been, your kids will grow up without ever getting to know you. They're already growing up in front of your eyes—it was just yesterday that you were holding them close and they were dependent on you for everything in life. Now they're growing older right in front of you, and you fear they'll be out of the house and have a family of their own before you ever really get a chance to be the parent you want to be.

You fear that the disconnection with your spouse might pull you apart. You're scared of what the future of your relationship will look like—whether you'll be able to stay together, to parent your children as partners. You worry that you may be left all alone one day, with only your work left to you.

I have a friend who is a pastor, and one of the services he provides in that role is being there with people at the end of their lives, to ease their passing. He's told me that people on their deathbed never say they wish they had worked more or that they wanted more balance. No, over and over again, people always say that they wish they had been able to connect even more with their families, with the people they loved most in the world.

I want to show you another way, so that at the end of your life you can look back with no regrets. I want you to know that you are not alone. You and so many other people are struggling with this false idea of balance—something that is absolutely unattainable for any significant length of time. And I want to give you permission to jump off the balance beam and never look back.

When you do, you will be able to fully experience life with your family—not just dinners and vacations, but having your spouse and kids realize the impact you're making on people through your work, so that they feel deeply *connected* to that impact. They will appreciate you and the work you do. Your children will be extremely proud of you, and they'll grow up to want to be just like you—to make an impact, just like they saw you make. You and your spouse will be connected more than ever before, and together you'll watch your children pursue higher education and careers as they move from adolescence to adulthood. You'll be able to connect with them within your lifetime—and then see the lifetime of impact *they* go on to make.

But all of that only becomes possible once you let go of the idea of work–life balance and instead learn to have work–life *harmony*.

IN HARMONY

I've heard so many people say, "I need better work–life balance." I want to change that mindset completely and instead help to create better work–life harmony for people who are leaders at work, in their communities, and at home—people just like you.

We will continue to examine how to pursue harmony throughout this book, but before we do, I want to look at a few reasons why seeking work–life balance simply does not work.

First, you're going after something that is impossible. You physically cannot maintain balance all the time; it's not sustainable over a lifetime. Eventually, you are going to fall out of balance. So why go after something that sets you up for a fall? Pursuing something that doesn't exist is foolish.

Second, most people who perpetuate the myth of work–life balance will tell you that, in order to maintain that balance, you have to work less or stop caring about work so much. That's not right at all! Work is beautiful, and we were created to contribute. You *like* to work, and you're good at it. You make an impact on people through your work, and that should never be stopped.

Third, we were also created to be in community. We were made to have relationships. When you invite different people into your song, and you are all on the same rhythm, pursuing everything in harmony, it creates a much better sense of community and oneness. No longer are you alone on the balance beam, juggling work and the other areas of your life. Instead, you are supported by loved ones across all areas of your life.

Finally, work–life balance implies that you have two lives, one for work and one for everything else. Are you attempting to sing two songs at once, one about work and one about life, each with its own rhythm, key, and tempo? It can't be done, and it's only going to lead to frustration—just like it's frustrating to try to believe that there are two parts to you, the work side and the *everything else* side. That simply isn't true.

You are one person, and you have one life. I'm not going to ask you to put on a different face for different parts of your life or to show up differently at home, at work, at church, or anywhere else. In fact, I am actually going to encourage you to simplify things by being the same person throughout the various areas of your life. You shouldn't have a separate song for work, for your family, for your friends, for your community, and for your hobbies; it's *all the same song*. Instead of trying to sing all those different songs at the same time—a recipe for a racket—the goal here is to invite all the areas of your life into one song, and then to sing it as beautifully and harmoniously as possible.

With a life of harmony, instead of the never-ending struggle to maintain a balancing act across all these warring parts of your life, each important area of focus in your life has a purpose, which allows them to work together to support and sustain each other. Instead of an overworked, hustle-and-grind mentality that takes over your home life and leaves your family resentful of the work that takes you away from them, maintaining work–life harmony means that everything ebbs and flows in a rhythm—a season for work, but a time for rest, too—and, most importantly, a connected family that is all a part of your overall life mission.

Doesn't that sound like music to your ears?

WHY THIS MATTERS

I strongly believe that we were created to contribute.

But it's difficult to keep contributing if we don't believe that the contributions we make are meaningful, impactful, and appreciated. On the other hand, if we stop contributing, it impacts our societies, the financial well-being of our communities, our homes, and the people we provide for.

The saddest part—the part that is *just plain wrong*—is that if you don't feel like you're contributing and being appreciated for that contribution, it affects your mental well-being. It impacts the joy and happiness you have in life.

You've likely experienced that feeling, and it *sucks*. So I want to change that. Not only do I want to help you achieve work–life harmony so you can have better relationships at home and at work, but I want you to have more joy in your life because you see, feel, believe, and understand that the work you're doing is making an impact. It's being fully appreciated by your peers, your team at work, and your family.

When everyone in your life truly appreciates the contributions you make, it makes those contributions and the effort you've made so much more sustainable. You don't feel alone. And you will add unbelievable amounts of joy and enjoyment to your life.

But how do I know this? Well, because other people *just like you* have told me.

After writing my first, bestselling book, *The Problem Isn't Their Paycheck: How to Attract Top Talent and Build a Thriving Company Culture*, I was invited to speak at conferences. Readers who had been helped with their teams in creating healthier company cultures followed me on social media. They heard me speak and saw me post about work, leadership, and finances—but also about my family and their support for all my endeavors. They saw that I have all these different companies—I own a mortgage company, an insurance agency, an investment management firm, and a software company—and yet, at least from the social media highlights, it appeared that I also have a family who loves me. (I absolutely do!)

And those readers reached out to me.

Messages poured in, in emails and direct messages, and every speaking event led to more and more face-to-face conversations with people. Almost all of them, even if they had initially reached out about management or leadership or hiring, ended up asking me about how I managed it— how I maintained work–life balance. "How? How do you do it all? How are you able to work in your businesses and still do awesome things with your family??"

And they told me about their personal lives. About the sadness, loneliness, and frustration. About their struggles and lack of enjoyment. They told me that they wanted to quit, that they just didn't see any other way. That their relationships were falling apart and they felt like they were failing, at home and at work, because there was never enough time for everything.

I listened to all of it. And I felt for them, just as I feel for you. My purpose in life, as you will learn in the next chapter, is to love people.

And that's why I wrote this book: to love people who are seeking balance but feeling like they can never get it right.

People like those I spoke to, emailed with, DMed in return. People like you.

This matters because you deserve to have work–life harmony, and all the joy and love that comes with it.

EXPECTATION MANAGEMENT

In this book, you are going to learn:

- That work is good, and you do not need to stop working (or work less) to have harmony
- How to create a meaningful purpose statement that you, your family, and your work can get on board with
- How to craft the ultimate work and family expectation management tool
- How to discover your quarterly, weekly, and daily rhythms so you can proactively get everyone on the same page
- Practical steps on how to rest, even in busy seasons, to help you be at your best
- How to grow and connect with the people you care about most, through evaluating and celebrating how well you are doing
- And how to enjoy life more because you have harmony!

So much of this book—of finding your purpose, inviting your family and your work into that purpose, of designing your ideal year, determining the rhythms of your life, learning how to rest well, and evaluating your progress—becomes more effective when expectations are well managed. Expectation management helps everybody get on the same page.

So I want to be a good steward for you as you read this book, and help manage your expectations. The first two chapters of this book represent a paradigm shift, an education and context that is absolutely necessary for you to thrive and find harmony. I want to give you that heads-up so you know what to expect, because it is vital that you read these two chapters first before progressing through the rest of the book—and I want you to be aware right up front so that you are able to read this book with success.

When I was writing this book, I considered narrowing those chapters or even moving them to the end so you could jump right into the action. But the truth is, you *need* to read them before you get to the remaining chapters, which are full of action steps, copy-and-paste examples, and other things you can do to implement more harmony in your life.

So that you don't feel frustrated as you process through this paradigm shift, I want to give you some quick wins. Between chapters, you'll see sections called "A Quick Win." These are short, fast action steps you can start doing now—right now, *today*—to experience a win. You'll see how much these add up to harmony as you continue reading the book, implementing everything else in it, and experiencing success.

You should also know that art is a practice. There's an art to harmony, and I'll teach you the processes and systems to have better harmony, so you can then practice it in your life. This is more than a book about a mindset shift. It includes tangible, real-life examples from my life and that of my family and employees. You will be able to see harmony in action and, by practicing what you learn, you will start to create harmony in your own life as well.

While this is going to be a learning experience, I don't want you to treat this book as a sacred text. Mark it up—get out your pen and circle or underline ideas that speak to you. Fold down the pages, highlight important points, and take notes. You'll even find space at the end of each chapter to fill in with your thoughts and action plans.

In fact, you don't even have to read this book yourself. You can find it on Audible, and I will read it to you! (And, spoiler alert, you'll even get to hear my wife as she reads "The Supportive Spouse" chapter.) If you do what I do and increase the reading pace to one-and-a-half or two times the speed, you'll go through the pages faster and will potentially retain more because you have to focus more. To level up your experience even more, try reading along in the book as you listen. This combination of visual and auditory learning will increase retention exponentially.

Dawson Trotman said, "Thoughts disentangle themselves when they pass through the lips and fingertips." You're going to think a lot as you're reading this book, and I want you to disentangle those thoughts by writing them down in the notes section. But I also want your thoughts to disentangle themselves by passing through your lips. Talk about your insights with friends, loved ones, employees or coworkers, and on social media. Share what you think harmony means and ask other people to share what *they* think in return. Reading a book like this doesn't have to be something you do in private. We are created for community, so have conversations and let what you learn help you feel less alone.

Even if you are at the very beginning of your journey, and that feels like a lonely place, you are not alone. Reach out with a picture or post on social media, tag me in it (@Grant-Botma on Twitter and Instagram), and find a community of other people who are starting to find harmony, just like you are.

Seriously: grab your phone, open Instagram or Twitter, and post a picture of yourself reading this book (or just the book if you're not into the whole selfie thing). Tag me in the photo, and I will do my absolute best to comment on the post or DM you so we can connect on social media.

REBUTTALS

As I've taught these ideas of work–life harmony to people, they've brought up questions and resistance they experienced when first learning of these ideas. As you read, you may experience some resistance as well. Because of this, you will see a section called Rebuttals at the end of each chapter, designed to help you overcome some of that resistance so you are free to find harmony in your life. Even if none of these FAQs directly apply to your situation, they will help you get a more complete understanding of how others absorb this information.

"Grant, I really tried—I've purchased all these books about work–life balance. I've listened to seminars and even hired business consultants or accountability coaches to try to help me, but I have a really hard time with it and I fail over and over again. So what's different about this? I don't want to fail again, and I don't want to start only to find that this is the same work–life balance stuff dressed up differently."

You failed because pursuing work–life balance sets you up for failure. You will fail every time, because you cannot stay balanced for your entire life. And I get it, you can't fail again.

So we're not going to have the goal of trying to stay balanced. I'm giving you a new target. Instead of going after something that doesn't exist, we're going to pursue something that doesn't exist, we're going to pursue something real and completely different: harmony.

When you pursue harmony, you don't have to choose your work or your life. It's all your life! And you might still make mistakes, but you will learn from them and do better the next time around. Most importantly, harmony will help you enjoy life more and give you greater connection to the people you want to spend that life with.

"You don't understand—I *can't* work less. My work has created my family's lifestyle, and I have to maintain that. We have goals for our future: going on vacation, buying a house, paying for our kids to go to college. We need to meet those goals, so I have to keep grinding to make that happen. If you're telling me to work less, this isn't going to work."

Let me be very clear here: I am not going to tell you to work less. Not at all. This is still *work*-life harmony, and the very first word there is "work."

But you are working toward goals, and behind those goals lies a purpose—the reason you work as hard as you do. In fact, we're going to dive into that even more in the next chapter, which is all about *purpose*. Keep reading.

RECITAL REVISITED

When your life is in harmony, it's the difference between that second-grade recital I asked you to imagine at the beginning of the Introduction...and going to see your child perform at their high school choir concert.

They have been practicing for years, so they're better at singing and so is everybody else on stage. You have that same sense of pride in seeing your child perform, but now it's even deeper because you know they have put in the necessary effort. And it makes for a completely different experience. Instead of hitting record, you are soaking it in. You're more engaged with the music, trying to take in every single detail, because each moment of this concert is absolutely beautiful.

Everybody in the choir sings in harmony. They are all on the same rhythm, moving in the same direction—even if they have different roles. At times, the altos and bass do a beautiful job of supporting the sopranos, who sing in a higher, angelic tone. Then the sopranos fade into the background and the bass comes in, singing with a low, almost humming noise that reverberates through your chest. It makes your heart start to vibrate with this completely different texture to the song. Finally, they all come together—altos, sopranos, baritones, and bass—to sing all at the same time. There's no other way of describing it than beauty. Even if you don't know the language the songs are sung in, you know it sounds gorgeous.

And although they all have different roles, they all understand each other. They know what everyone else on stage is going to do next. Everybody working together, supporting each other's roles, is what allows them to make this beautiful harmony.

And that's what I want for your life.

I want you to have an unbelievably beautiful experience in this one life that you have. Instead of going after balance, you can have harmony, just like the choir singers who all know what to expect from one another because they are on the same page and understand how to support each other.

By reading this book, you will learn to have work–life harmony, which when done well—and with a little practice—makes your life an even more beautiful song.

KEY TAKEAWAYS

- Grab a pen and keep it handy, so you can highlight, underline, and write down your thoughts as you read.
- Follow me on Twitter and/or Instagram, @GrantBotma, and I'll do my best to respond and engage with you.
- Take a picture, either a selfie of yourself with this book or a picture of the cover of the book, and post it on social media. Don't forget to tag me!

MY INTENTIONAL ACTIONS

....

....

....

....

....

....

....

....

....

....

....

....

....

A QUICK WIN: ONE KID UP

Once a week, my wife, Jodie, and I pick an evening to let one of our children stay up with us while the other two go to bed at their usual bedtime. We rotate which kid gets to stay up, and whichever is the One Kid Up gets to stay up, just that one kid with the attention of both parents.

The whole point of One Kid Up is to spend some special time with each kid, without their siblings around. Sometimes we just sit and watch TV, and they get to pick the show they want to watch. They get their own snuggle time with Mommy and Daddy, which is very precious to us, and they love it too!

Other times, we'll have intentional conversations, educating them about sex, drugs, alcohol, and other topics. We start talking about these topics with our kids at an early age because we know that the world is going to introduce them to these things, but we want to control those conversations as much as possible.

Sometimes they'll choose a dessert they want and we'll make them together. Or they pick a game or puzzle for us to do, just the three of us. Other times, *they* have stuff they want to talk to us about, or questions they want to ask, like, "What was life like when you were little?" Or, "Why did you guys get married?" That's their opportunity to have our focused attention, just on them.

If you have kids, give this a try. Let one kid stay up, even if it's just a little later than normal. Or have your other kids go to their rooms a little early; if they're not tired, they don't have to sleep, but they have to stay in their room. Ask your One Kid Up what they want to do, and follow their lead.

The cool part is that this doesn't have to take a bunch of extra time out of your already busy week. It usually takes less than an hour—but your kids will feel like it is the *most special* time. Instead of doing a load of laundry or jumping back into work—whatever the post-bedtime routine looks like in your household—take one hour a week to give each of your kids a little extra attention and let them feel like the star.

(Again, if even that hour a week feels overwhelming, consider sending the other kids to their rooms an hour earlier, so this takes *no* time away from your usual nighttime routine.)

CHAPTER 1

PURPOSE

My purpose is to love others. When I tell people that, they often ask me, "Grant, how did you discover your purpose?"

I came to discover my purpose by reading the Bible.

I grew up going to church, but when I was in college I began challenging things, trying to figure out, *Is this real?* All that stuff people had been telling me in church, and everything that was written in the Bible—was it legit?

As I tried to disprove what I'd learned, I actually ended up validating it. Ultimately, I became attracted to God's word and the teachings of Jesus so much that I thought to myself, "The Bible is big. There's a lot to it, and I don't understand it all, so I'm just going to focus on determining one answer: what's the most important thing here?"

In trying to determine the most important *thing* in the Bible, I first had to focus on the most important *person*. That's easy: Jesus.

So then I started reading to figure out the most important thing Jesus said. After all, if He's the most important person in the Bible, then the most important thing He said is probably the most important thing overall in the Bible.

I asked myself, "If I were Jesus, when would I likely say the most profound thing?" Probably right before I died or knew I was going to leave this planet.

After Jesus died and rose again, just before He ascended into Heaven, He told his disciples, "Go, therefore, and make disciples of all the nations, baptizing them in the name of the Father and the Son and the Holy Spirit, teaching them to follow all that I commanded you; and behold, I am with you always, to the end of the age."[1]

The church has determined this quote, called the Great Commission, to be incredibly important.

But I wanted to go even deeper.

So if this is potentially the most important thing ever said or written in the history of the planet...what's *the most import-*

---

1   Matthew 28:19–20

ant word in this Bible verse? Well, when I first looked at what Jesus said and tried to determine the most important word, I thought it was "go." Go is a verb, an action word.

Some people say the most important word is "disciple" because that is what Jesus hopes for people to become. Others think that "baptizing" is the most important word because that means telling people about Jesus and converting them to become followers of Christ.

None of those felt right to me, though.

And then I remembered Ms. Klomparence, my seventh-grade teacher. She had a beehive hairdo and wingtip glasses. She was really old with wrinkly skin, and would whack you with a ruler if you got an answer wrong. She was frustrating to have as a teacher, but I remember how to dissect sentences because of her class—even though, at the time, all I thought was, "Why are you teaching me this? I'll never need to know this!"

Ms. Klomparence taught me that, grammatically speaking, the most important word of a sentence is its subject. In the Great Commission, the subject is "them." In fact, it's not even a sentence—or a complete thought—without that word. *Them.*

Who are we going to? Them. Who are we making disciples of? Them. Who are we baptizing? Them.

I remembered another verse: "Even the Son of Man did not come to be served, but to serve others and to give His life as ransom for many."[2]

Jesus didn't just say this stuff; he *lived it*. He made his whole life about others. That's when it all clicked into place. *My life needs to be about* them.

So that's what my life is about. And not only is that my purpose, but I also want to invite you, as you're reading this book, to make *your* purpose about *them* too. If you also believe that you can make your purpose about others, then guess what? You're following along with what countless people throughout the history of the planet have decided to make their lives about: others. Life is about them.

And my purpose in life is to love them.

In all honesty, that's what I believe everybody's purpose in life is—but I can't tell you your purpose. You have to agree to it. You have to believe it for yourself.

I'm not sure where you are in your relationship with religion, Jesus, or the Bible, so my story of how I discovered my purpose may not resonate with you at all—and *that's okay*. No matter your worldview or life outlook, all the information I share in this book is applicable to you. You don't have to be

---

2   Mark 10:45

Christian, have a relationship with Jesus, or read the Bible to have a purpose—or to get value from the information you are going to learn.

Regardless of your outlook on religion, I think we can all agree that having a life purpose that is focused on others makes the world a better place.

THE IMPORTANCE OF PURPOSE

Your purpose is necessary for work–life harmony; you can't have work–life harmony without it. Once you have your purpose, you invite your family, your work, your church, and all the different areas of your life into that purpose. (More on this in Chapter 2!)

Where people get messed up, usually when trying to pursue work–life balance, is thinking that different aspects of life have different purposes. Those people try to pursue all of those different purposes all at the same time, attempting to juggle everything at once. They end up back on the balance beam, bouncing from one to the other, attempting to meet all these purposes—and trying not to fall off.

If you don't have a purpose, you have nothing to invite people into—no goal that everybody is on the same page to pursue; no key that everybody in the band is playing together. However, when you recognize that you have *one life* with *one purpose* that everything else is invited into, everything is headed in the same direction.

When you discover your purpose, life becomes simpler. Everything you do in your life needs to point to that purpose. For me, my whole life points to my purpose: loving them.

If I have a big decision to make, I run it through the filter of my life purpose. Hypothetically, if I were to be offered a job and had to figure out whether or not to take it, I'd ask myself, "Does it allow me to love them?" If so, great! That's a job I can get behind. What if I'm offered two jobs, and I have to decide which one to take? Well, which one allows me to love them better? I'll take that one.

Should I marry this woman? I don't know, is she going to help me love them better? Should we have kids right now? If we have kids, is that going to allow us to love them better? Sure it is. It's going to teach us more about people. It's going to help us learn to sacrifice better. And it's going to give us an opportunity to teach more people—our kids—how to love them better. Let's do it!

My purpose is a simple thing that I can point to, to help with my decision-making, which makes life so much simpler. And when life is simpler, and you have one thing that your life is about, you are singing that one beautiful song. My song is called "Love Them."

But if you're reading this and you don't currently have a purpose (or you don't yet know what it is), *that's okay*. Don't stop reading, and don't feel like you've failed. We're going to walk through how to create a purpose statement together.

And if you *do* already have a purpose but you're not confident about it, by the time you're done reading this chapter you'll have created something strong to believe in, a purpose that you can live your life for.

This book is not about giving you a purpose in life; I don't want you to believe that, as you keep reading, you are going to find your purpose. Instead, you're going to create a purpose statement around a purpose you already know you have but haven't been able to put words to.

If you are searching to find your purpose, I highly recommend reading one of the bestselling books of all time, other than the Bible: *The Purpose Driven Life* by Rick Warren. I think you'll find it helpful.

HOW TO CREATE YOUR PURPOSE STATEMENT

I have come up with a simple way to create your purpose statement. It involves answering just four questions.

QUESTION 1: WHAT PROBLEMS ARE IN THE WORLD?

The first question to consider when creating your purpose statement is, *What problems are in the world*?

Write down problems you see and recognize in the world. (There are likely going to be a lot of them!) As you write down these problems, you can begin to organize them into three categories:

1. External problems: ones that everybody sees (for example, that someone is going hungry)
2. Internal problems: the internal battle that occurs within your mind as a result of that external problem; how it makes an individual feel (for example, when somebody is hungry, they are unable to focus, their mind and body can't perform how they need to)
3. Philosophical problems: larger-scale societal issues that people can rally around; answer the question "Why is that problem *just plain wrong*?" (It is *just plain wrong* that an individual who is going hungry can't be at their best because they can't contribute to society or make a positive impact on the world, so they can't fulfill their life's purpose.)

Ideally, your purpose statement doesn't just deal with external, or even only internal, problems. The philosophical piece is the most important part of a problem to be solved, because it motivates more people and has a higher impact when solved, so it's better if your life purpose can deal with philosophical problems. Why is the problem you see *just plain wrong*? Creating a purpose statement around answering this question will make that statement more meaningful and sustainable.

QUESTION 2: WHAT DO I WANT TO DO ABOUT IT?

The second question to ask yourself is, *What do I want to do about it?*

You understand that there's a problem, you've focused on the philosophical aspect of it, but what do you want to *do* about it? It could be that you want to help, you want to encourage, you want to love. You may want to educate, minister, or disciple. What are the things that you want to do? Do you want to give, to connect, to create, to nourish? Think about what you can do about that problem and what action you are going to take to help solve that problem.

QUESTION 3: WHO AM I GOING TO SERVE?

The third question is, *Who am I going to serve?*

Who are the people who have this problem? For me, it might be people in my hometown of Gilbert, or people in the state of Arizona, people in the United States, or in the world. For you, the people you're going to serve may be in a certain town or state or a specific country. Maybe it's a certain group of people, like your family, or possibly it's just people in general.

QUESTION 4: WHAT OUTCOME AM I GOING TO PROVIDE?

And the fourth and final question is, *What outcome am I going to provide?*

Are you going to provide a full stomach? A sense of belonging? The ability to flourish and thrive? Will you provide happiness or freedom? What are you going to provide to the people you're going to serve, through what you're doing?

PUT THEM ALL TOGETHER

My life purpose is to "love them."

What's the problem? People need to be loved. It's just plain wrong when they're not loved because then they start acting out of selfishness. And when selfishness is acted on, the world is a much worse place to live. I believe people were created in this world to give and receive love and when they don't receive love, things don't go well.

So what am I going to do? I am going to love.

Who am I going to love? I'm going to love them.

And what's the outcome going to be? It's going to be *love*.

It seems super simple. Love them. And it just so happens that one word—love—matches three of the four questions here.

Your life purpose may be to create a world where everyone belongs. It looks simple, but it answers the four questions.

What's the problem? People don't have a sense of belonging.

What do you want to do? You want to create.

Who are you going to serve? The world.

And what's the outcome? Everyone is going to belong.

EVALUATE YOUR PURPOSE

My life purpose, as you have seen, is to love people.

When creating a life purpose statement, you don't need to write some big, long, convoluted paragraph. Your purpose should be selfless and simple, so it's easy to invite people into.

SELFLESS

This sounds counterintuitive, but your life purpose shouldn't be about you. It's not something that tries to make your life sound bigger, better, or stronger. As Simon Sinek said, "No matter how much money we make, no matter how much power we accumulate, no matter how many promotions we're given, none of us will ever be declared the winner of life."

Your purpose needs to be outside of yourself. It needs to be selfless. If it's not—if you have a selfish purpose—you are going to have a really hard time inviting others into your purpose and getting your work and your family to be in harmony with you.

When you make your purpose, and your life, about others— when you are concerned about others ahead of concern for yourself, and you try to help others, being generous with your finances, resources, and time—it actually increases your happiness. Not only will having a selfless life purpose allow you to invite others in, to pursue this purpose with you, but selfless people are also statistically proven to be happier.

Think about people you know who are self-centered or who seek selfish pursuits. Do you enjoy hanging out with those people?

Now think about people in your life who are incredibly

generous, whether with their resources, time, wisdom, or attention. They are selfless and genuinely care about other people. Wouldn't you rather hang out with them?

> This is a great opportunity to let your thoughts disentangle themselves through your lips and fingertips. Why don't you send a message to that person you really appreciate? Let them know, "Hey, I consider you to be a selfless and generous person, and I just want to let you know that I think you're awesome." That's a great way to encourage somebody!

The best way to determine if your life purpose is selfless is to ask, "Does it require me to sacrifice?" If you have to give something up or serve, there's a good chance that your purpose is selfless.

SIMPLE

Your life purpose should also be simple.

It does not need to have thirty-dollar words. It shouldn't be multiple sentences long—or one long, run-on sentence. It shouldn't be a paragraph. In fact, you shouldn't even need to write it down in order to remember it—that's how simple it should be.

The purpose you're creating should be simple so that it's easy to invite other people into it. If someone asks me,

"What's your life about?" I can reply, "I'm here on the planet to love people." That's simple *and* it invites people to want to learn more.

BONUS QUESTION

The final aspect of your life's purpose is to ask whether it gets you emotionally charged up. Does it feel like you? Do you believe it? You can't just have a purpose statement that sounds neat, or because I have one. You have to believe it.

This is not a matter of taking three minutes to answer these questions as quickly as possible and then moving on to the next chapter. You have to be really honest with yourself and examine something bigger than you. This does not work unless you first look in the mirror and admit some difficult truths: "I'm selfish at times—and that's okay. I'm humble enough to admit it, and I'm willing to do as much as I can to fix it."

That's hard to do. The truth is that when we have an issue in our lives, whether it be in a relationship, at work, or at home, I can guarantee that there is some source of selfishness involved somewhere in that problem.

Selfishness, being brash and rude, pushing your way through things, and constantly competing can be helpful at times, but they're not sustainable behaviors. The longest-lasting and highest-quality relationships exist because humility and selflessness are involved.

You can still be confident *and* humble. In fact, these are the qualities of an excellent leader. When you're an excellent leader who acts with selflessness and humility, you have earned the right to invite people into this song that you're singing to get in harmony with you—and people will also ask to sing the song with you! People will pursue you, to be a part of this purpose with you, because it's so attractive.

The people you're enjoying life with, that you're creating that harmony with, are your people, the people who are part of that purpose. They're people who think and feel like you and who want to pursue that purpose with you. You're a more attractive person because you're making your life about others. You had to have a humble moment to get to this place, and humility is attractive.

Your life purpose gives your daily actions direction and meaning while at the same time eliminating loneliness.

You have a reason to wake up in the morning. You're making an impact in the world. You're contributing, because all your actions and everything you do in your life is pointing toward this purpose and the contribution that you're making to the world. And that allows you to leave the world better than it was when you came into it.

Instead of being alone, flailing your arms on the balance beam, you're locking arms with other people. You share a goal. And now you sing with one voice, in harmony. You're not alone anymore.

REBUTTALS

At the beginning of this chapter, I told you the story of how I discovered my life purpose. But you may have been wounded from church in the past, so you may be thinking something like, **"I've seen/experienced some really crappy stuff in the world."** Or you may be saying, **"Hey, Grant, that's all well and good but I'm an atheist; I don't believe in God."** Or, **"I'm agnostic, and I'm not really sure what's out there."**

The concepts in this book ring true for everybody, regardless of your religion or relationship with God. Although I have a relationship with Jesus and I am a Christian, you do not need to be a Christian to apply the concepts here and achieve work–life harmony.

For those of you who have been hurt by church, or who have experienced pain in your life that has pushed you away from Christianity, religion, or a relationship with God, I'm sorry, and I love you. I want you to know that I am genuinely sorry you've experienced that hurt; I wish you never had. I can say that with an empathetic heart because I've been hurt too, and I know many people who have been hurt, and it doesn't feel great. I'm sorry.

I promise that if you continue reading this book, you're going to get value from this regardless of your religious affiliation or relationship with our Creator. Even if you remove the religion piece from this—if you remove my Christian religion from this purpose—I think we can all agree that making life about more than just yourself is going to result in a happier life.[3]

And you can still create a life purpose statement without the religious angle. If you don't want to create one like I did, by going through scripture, you can still follow the framework, which works no matter where you're at in your work in life and religion. It doesn't matter if you have a relationship with Jesus or not; the only way to have work–life harmony is to create a life purpose that is simple, selfless, and easy to invite others into.

"Grant, I can't do this. I'm not that important, or I can't make that big an impact."

You're wrong. You are important and you can make an impact, because you're here. If you're here, if you're waking up and still breathing, you have purpose. You have an

---

3   https://www.psychologytoday.com/us/blog/between-cultures/201805/
    in-helping-others-you-help-yourself

amazing opportunity. It doesn't matter what you've done or what's been done to you—you can still make a positive impact on this world.

It's not about trying to reconcile the mistakes you've made, no matter what they are, or about trying to right the wrongs you've experienced. It just means trying to do the best with what you've got. I want to invite you into that.

You *are* important. And you are here for a reason.

"Grant, I'm having a hard time creating this purpose statement. I don't know if I should continue reading this book."

Yes, absolutely. Keep going! There is plenty more for you to learn. You already experienced a quick win from the exercise before this chapter, and the book is filled with more, very simple resources you can apply that will help you get better at work–life harmony.

If creating your purpose statement feels too hard or like it is too much, you're overthinking it.

I understand that you want a grandiose, unbelievably wonderful purpose statement that sends chills down your spine and genuinely motivates you to take every step of your life with crazy amounts of joy and smiles. You may even want to create a purpose statement that brings tears to your eyes when you read it. Here's the hard truth: it doesn't always do that, and that's okay. Life isn't like that. Those big emotions are so precious because they're rare. You may experience that type of connection with your purpose as you live it out, but the likelihood that you're going to experience this overwhelming emotion as you create it isn't very high.

It's simple. Don't overthink it. Don't try to create an emotional moment. Just go through the exercise; it's four simple steps. Anyone can do it.

And if you've done it and you don't like the purpose statement you created, that's okay too. You can edit it or change it. That doesn't mean it was wrong.

"Grant, this is way bigger than I thought a book about work-life harmony was going to be. This life purpose is too big for me."

This book is created to offer a paradigm shift. If you're not aligned with that yet, there are also some practical, step-by-step, copy-and-paste resources that worked for me. We'll get to those in the very next chapter!

And, hey, I get it. I'm a busy guy—I own a mortgage company, an insurance agency, an investment management firm, and a software company, and we won Inc. 5000's

Fastest-Growing Companies in America twice. I wrote one bestselling book, and I'm writing this one. I have a wife and three kids, and together we help take care of my disabled brother-in-law—and they still love me. On top of all of that, I am still able to take two months "off" during the year.

If I can do it, you can do it. And learning how I did it, through my purpose, is a big part of it. But even if you're not there quite yet, keep reading, because I'm sure you'll be able to pick up the rest of it.

This book is intentionally designed for you to be able to read it more than once. You've read this far, so pause and absorb whatever your thoughts and feelings are here. Write them in the notes section at the end of the chapter. Every book is going to be made more effective if you read it more than once—it doesn't matter if it's this book or another one. You should be reading books more than once because you'll get something new out of them each time or be able to apply more because you have a different and better understanding of it. Talk to people in your life about it to take that understanding even deeper.

The paradigm shift has already started. You've read the first chapter of the book. When you read it again, you get to shift again, but the distance to move is much smaller than when you were first introduced to the concept.

Keep going. If you're looking for practical advice for finding harmony, you will find it here. If you're not sure yet, you can come back to this chapter.

INVITE THEM IN

My purpose is to love them. In my family, we believe we are here to love others. Likewise, I live out my purpose at work by loving people through finances. See how they're all connected?

That's because I've invited my work and my family into my purpose.

You've created your purpose statement to be simple, so it's easy to invite others into it. In the next chapter, we'll look at just how to do that—just like you would invite your band to practice every day, to make harmony.

KEY TAKEAWAYS

- Create your purpose statement by answering four questions:
  - What problems are in the world?
  - What do you want to do about it?
  - Who are you going to serve?
  - What outcome are you going to provide?
- Make sure your purpose is selfless and simple, so it's easy to invite others into it.
- Finally, do a gut check to make sure your purpose feels like *you*. You have to believe in it so much that you are willing to point everything in your life toward that purpose.

MY INTENTIONAL ACTIONS

A QUICK WIN: SAY THANK YOU

Now that you've created this purpose, think about times in your life when your purpose has been achieved. Think about times you've succeeded and made part of your life about more than just yourself, or you've helped others win or achieve a win. Think back on any recent workplace success you've had. Maybe that means an award, an additional commission or bonus you qualified for, recognition from your boss, or a really great review left by a customer.

Think about the impact you made on others and how your purpose was being lived out in that moment, in that area of your life.

Now think of somebody in your life who helped you meet that purpose. Who is someone without whom you could not have achieved what you did? Whether they know it or not, if they hadn't been part of your life, it wouldn't have happened. This may be your spouse, a child, your parents, a friend, or someone in your life who laid the groundwork to help you become the person you are in that moment: a teacher, coach, pastor, aunt, or uncle.

Maybe you have many people who helped you live out that purpose; think of at least one. And then tell them *thank you*. Let them know that you couldn't have done it without them. That it was their love, support, and care for you that allowed you to do this—their kisses and snuggles, that word of encouragement, a home-cooked meal in the evening during that really hard week, and their having grace for you when you were unable to show up as much as you wanted to. Thank them for any sacrifice they made to help you be the person you needed to be during that time when you performed in such a way that you won that award or accolade. Let them know that praise isn't just yours—it's theirs, too.

If it wasn't for them and the time they poured into you, you wouldn't have been able to achieve this success, and their support impacted a lot of other people. This gives your loved ones a greater appreciation for what you're doing and lets them know that their sacrifices aren't for nothing; it goes toward a greater purpose that is being lived out.

CHAPTER 2

INVITE YOUR FAMILY AND YOUR WORK INTO YOUR LIFE PURPOSE

Even if you're the lead singer in a band, you know that there are times when you are going to have a solo and other times when you will sing along with the background singers. Sometimes other players will have a solo, and that's when you step back and let them take the stage.

Every member of the band has a role, and each of those roles is important to support harmony.

But this can be easy to forget.

When my children were very young, my family and I went to Disneyland. While we were there, we sat on the curb of Main Street to watch a parade going by. My kids were entranced by the lights and colors, songs and characters, staring up with their mouths open and their eyes wide.

As they were watching, I was on the phone with someone for work, having a pretty heated conversation. Something I yelled attracted my kids' attention, even over the sounds and sights of the parade. Their mouths snapped shut and their eyes got even bigger. They were worried!

That brought me up short. *"What am I doing?"* I wondered.

Here in this magical place, designed for children's happiness, my kids were distracted by wondering what was going on with me and why I was so upset.

In that moment, I wasn't living out my life's purpose of loving them.

PURPOSE + FAMILY + WORK = HARMONY

The people closest to you—your spouse, kids, family, and friends—probably have no idea how hard you work or how good you are at your job. And if that's true, they likely have no idea how much of an impact you make on the people in your community every day.

I want to remove the shame you may have about work. Work is *good*. It's okay to love what you do and to take pride in your work. Work–life harmony is not about telling you to work less or to stop working.

Work is probably really fulfilling for you, but your spouse and kids may not understand what it is you do all day, so they ask, "Why don't we go on vacation more often?" Or, "Why don't we go on more dates?" Or even, "I need more time with you."

Without a purpose helping to create harmony, you're not on the same page as your spouse and kids. Your kids, at times, resent you. You end up apologizing to your family: "I'm sorry, guys, I can't do that. I have to go to work." When you leave the house for the day, they say, "Ugh, you have to work *again*?!"

When you hear that, you likely bite your tongue, thinking of how hard you work. But, eventually, you just can't bite your tongue any longer...and then you snap. You might say something like, "Do you have any idea how hard I work for you?! How do you think we pay for this house, our cars, or your private school?"

This is a common conversation in many households, and it leads to countless issues because the family is so disconnected from the work being done by other members of the household that the work is seen as not important or not valuable. *And when the work you're doing isn't valued by your family, how are you supposed to get the support you need to do that work?*

You don't want your spouse and kids to resent the work you do or the time you spend at the office. You want your family to see you, to see what you do, and to support you. Instead of nagging, you need cheerleaders who tell you, "Go kick butt and have an awesome day pursuing that purpose. I'm proud of you!"

When you connect your work and family to your purpose, your children will celebrate you when you leave the house to go to work—not because you're leaving but because they want to cheer you on for the impact you are going to have in the lives of other people. When I leave in the morning, I say, "Okay, kids, I'm going to work. I'm going to love people through finances today." And they respond, "Go get 'em, Dad!" Or, "I'll be praying for you today, Dad! I hope it goes really well."

When you come home from work, your kids will ask you about your day because they're excited to find out what's going on at work. They want to see that purpose being fulfilled and hear stories of the impact you made on people.

Because of this connection, your spouse will also be more

supportive. When busy seasons arise—and they do, especially when you're good at your job—instead of stress, anxiety, or complaints when you have some more work to do after putting the kids to bed, your spouse might bring you a cold drink or massage your shoulders to help you relax.

When you win at work, you don't win by yourself. You get to celebrate it with your family and enjoy it together. You bring them joy and smiles and happiness. Because you have their support while you're pursuing this purpose, work becomes even more meaningful.

And you yourself have a different mindset. Instead of feeling guilty for busy times at work or for wanting to spend time with your family, you now have this purpose. You're living it at work and sharing it with your children. You're supported in it by your spouse. Everything you do—whether at work or with your family or anything else in your life—becomes easier and requires less effort because it has meaning. It has *purpose*.

But how do you go from resentment and nagging to turning your family into your biggest cheerleaders and most ardent supporters? By inviting your family and your work, together, into your purpose. That is the key to creating work-life harmony.

Remember, we're not pursuing work-life balance, which

dictates, "Spend more time here, spend less time there." I'm not here to tell you what to do with your time, because work–life harmony has nothing to do with how much time you spend at work or how much time you spend with your family. It's about inviting both your family and your work into this amazing purpose you are pursuing in your *life*.

No longer do you have a work life and home life. You have one life.

The reason most people feel like they have a work life and a home life is because they live those two lives separately. They're not present in their home life. Their most cherished relationships have no idea what's going on at work.

But when you invite your work and your family into your life purpose, that separation disappears and you are left with harmony. It's time for you and your family to stand for something, to live for something, to point all actions toward a goal, so you're all moving in the same direction together.

The first step is to be clear on how your work connects to your purpose by creating a work purpose statement. Once you have these words, it will be easier to share them with your family so you can have meaningful conversations about how all of you contribute to your shared purpose in life.

CREATE A WORK PURPOSE STATEMENT

Malcolm Gladwell said, "Hard work is a prison sentence only if it does not have meaning."

Let me be clear: your life already has meaning. But when you have purpose in your work, it gives life *even more* meaning. This is true for two reasons: one, every business is fundamentally created to serve someone, somewhere. It's not a business without providing a service or product that helps people in some way. And the best way to serve somebody is to put their needs ahead of your own, so self-lessness wins in business every time. That right there shows that working inherently provides a purpose in life that is about others. It's about something you can do that's outside of yourself.

And the second reason work gives life meaning is because we were created to contribute. It feels good to do good work because we were created for this. Work is a praiseworthy endeavor.

Yes, work is going to be hard at times. But it becomes easier when you are tied deeply to the meaning work provides.

In fact, the meaning of work is less about the actual work you do and more about your mindset. To get clearer on that mindset, and to connect your work with your purpose—or the reason you get up and serve every day—it is useful to create a work purpose statement.

My work purpose statement is to love people through finances. I own a company called Stewardship where we do home loans, insurance, and investments with wisdom and love. We serve people through their finances because we want to take care of them.

To begin crafting your work purpose statement, ask yourself the following questions:

- What is the purpose you're fulfilling every day?
- Who are the people you are making an impact on?
- What type of impact are you making on them?
- How are you making their world a better place?

And before you protest because you think the work you do is trivial, you are wrong. As an example, you may say something like, "Well, I don't make the world a better place because all I do is make sandwiches," you're thinking about it wrong. You have to go deeper than that to find your purpose. It's more than just making the sandwich; it's about what happens as a result of the service and product you're providing. That sandwich you make nourishes people. It gives them the calories and energy they need to put forth their effort in serving other people in their lives.

The sandwich I ate for lunch yesterday was amazing. It gave me just the boost I needed to write a chapter of this book and to do the other things I need to do in order to love people through finances. Without that sandwich, I would have been hungry and cranky. I wouldn't have been able to focus. And I certainly would not have been able to love people through their finances as well as I did. That's a fact.

So you have to look past "just" a sandwich, to ask what that sandwich does—and then what does it do after that?

When many people think about their work purpose, they tend to get caught up in the details. I want to encourage you to keep taking it deeper. What does the person you serve do with the thing you gave them, whether it's a sandwich or a cell phone or financial advice? How does what you provide them impact their life? And how do they impact other people's lives from there? If you keep going down this big chain reaction, you will see a huge purpose in what you do at work. The heart of creating a work purpose is evaluating the impact made on people—not just on the surface, but several layers deep.

Once that impact is clear, it's time to share it with the people closest to you: your family.

FAMILY + PURPOSE IN ACTION

I asked my oldest daughter, Cambria, to write a letter about what she thinks I do at work and how that ties in with what life is about. Here's what she wrote:

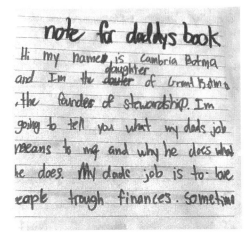

The letter says:

note for daddys book

*Hi my name is Cambria Botma and Im the daughter of Grant
Botma, the founder of stewardship. Im going to tell you what my
dads job means to me and why he does what he does. My dads
job is to love people trough finances. Sometimes I dont always
understand what his job is but he always tells me that "life is
about others and what do we do with others...love" so he told me
that is what he does at work. I do know my dad helps people with
money and gives them wise advise about what to do with there
money also he helps them to give, save, and spend.*

As you can see, I didn't correct any of what she wrote. She
may have said things differently than I would have, but this
is her authentic take on what I do and what life is about. It is
a real-life example of what it looks like to invite your family
and your work into your purpose.

This letter is straight from Cambria's heart, and I'm very
proud of her. She is currently twelve years old, and I'm proud
of how she's able to articulate herself and that she's willing
and able to communicate my purpose at work and with our
family. I'm proud of her confidence and that she knows what
life is about. She also wrote that she doesn't always understand what I do, and that's okay. She doesn't need to know
what it means to manage investments or anything like that.

Connecting your work and your family to your purpose doesn't mean that your family understands exactly how you do what you do; it means that your family knows *why* you do what you do and, as a result, what they need to do to support you.

Because my daughter knows how my work connects to our family purpose, she has grace for me in the times when I have to work a lot and get home late at night. On days when I have a particularly full workload, she might take time to snuggle with me a little extra and ask me questions about what's going on at work to make sure I'm doing okay.

Cambria has this level of understanding—as do our other two children—because my wife and I are very intentional about connecting my work purpose with our family purpose. We have a lot of conversations around this. From the time our kids were young, I never said, "Sorry, Daddy has to go to work," in a sad, apologetic tone. I never talked about work like it's something getting in the way of spending time with my wife and children.

I always talk about work as an opportunity to serve and love other people. When I'm walking out the door in the morning, I say something like, "Guess what, guys? I have the opportunity to serve and love people through their finances. I'm going to help so many people today." Sometimes I'll even show my kids the calendar app on my phone so they can see the appointments I have for the day. "Today I get to help John Doe. I'm going to meet with him, and I think we're going to talk about what he can do this year to better protect the money he has worked so hard to earn, and I'm going to help him and give him advice." I share that with them so they are bought in. When I get home, they ask, "Hey, Dad, how was your day at work? Were you able to help Mr. Doe?"

I'm also candid when I have a tough day, sharing with my kids that I feel like I didn't do a good job or why it was hard. I've even said, "If I'm honest with you, I don't feel like going to work today. But I know it's the right thing to do. I need to go and love people through finances, because if I don't then this (negative thing) will happen."

The conversations are very intentional, to show who I get to love through finances, because that ties to our family's purpose of loving others.

LIVING YOUR PURPOSE AT HOME

Having a purpose helps with parenting. When my kids are fighting or there are issues in our house, the most frequent cause is selfishness. Well, we have a family purpose that is about loving others, so whenever they do something wrong, I can say, "Hey, what is life about?" and they recite, "Others."

"And what are you supposed to do to others?"

"Love."

"Okay, is this behavior a good example of loving others?"

"No."

They talk about it with me and it creates a conversation about what they did that they shouldn't have done, with purpose rather than shame or blame. Having a purpose that is others-focused rather than self-focused helps resolve a lot of problems that come up. Loving others and having a selfless, others-centered purpose means that you're going to have a household with a lot less conflict.

It not only creates a way to course correct, but it also helps you give accolades and encouragement to keep going in that right direction. When they do something awesome, I can say, "Hey, that right there was so loving to others. That was great!"

As a family with purpose, you also get to celebrate together. You might say to your spouse and kids, "Hey, we're going to go on vacation! And one of the reasons why we get to do this is because we did a great job loving others. We're going to celebrate some of these awesome things we did together!" Instead of just being a parent who says, "We're going on vacation because we need to spend time with each other," you give it deeper meaning. You celebrate meeting your purpose—*and* you spend time together.

Finally, connecting your family with your purpose makes it easier to do hard things. When you and your family are doing hard things, it means you're sacrificing. You're being selfless. Having a purpose that's others-focused makes it part of your family culture. It becomes what other people know your family for.

People know that when they come into our household and engage with us, they will be loved. They can count on us to serve people, to take care of people, to be generous, and to love others. So that means we're helping other people and having a positive impact on their lives.

CONSISTENT CONVERSATION

Inviting your family and your work into your purpose doesn't have to mean holding a grand inquisition meeting with your family. It's not you grandstanding and telling your spouse and kids, "Okay, guys, here's what we're going to do from now on."

It takes multiple back-and-forth conversations. I've found that the best conversations tend to happen at mealtimes, when we're all sitting around the dinner table and talking.

That means being intentional about mealtimes, making them about more than filling your body with nutrients; much more than that, mealtime can be a community event to bring your family closer together.

When you are asked "How was your day?" or ask it of others, be intentional about the answers. When my family asks me about my day, I tell them the actions I took to help love people through their finances—or I explain what happened in my workday that prevented me from doing that, and why it was frustrating or challenging.

When I ask my kids about their day, I ask follow-up questions based on what they say to tie it into our family purpose. I might say, "Ellenie, beautiful job loving others today," or, "Hey, Parker, it sounds like you're having a tough situation with your friends. Any ideas of how you could maybe love them better tomorrow?"

Take the natural conversation that happens at the dinner table and, instead of keeping it at the surface level, create a conversation that has a bigger impact focused around your purpose. *This* is what takes your purpose from just being words on paper or painted on the wall to actually putting it into action. This is how we live it out.

If you are trying this out for the first time, you may want to do something outside of a regular meal. Maybe you want to prepare something special or take your family out to eat and say, "Hey guys, I'm taking us out for this nice meal because I want to talk about my work purpose and how it fits in with our family purpose." Create a memory or do something a little different from what you normally do to initiate or shift that conversation.

Having said that, this is not a one-and-done conversation just because you have it over steak and lobster. It's a perpetual conversation. It makes sense to continue this conversation at regular mealtimes because you have to eat every day, and it's a natural time for families to share details about their day.

Now, does this conversation have to happen every day? Do I tell my kids about what I did to love people through finances every time we eat dinner? No. I'm lucky if we get the chance to do that three times out of the seven nights a week. Sometimes people in our family have different things going on and we don't get the chance to eat dinner together. Sometimes we have other things to talk about, and that's okay.

If you haven't been talking about your purpose at all, and you start talking about it even once a week, that's a big deal. Over time, you can even start changing your question from, "How was your day?" to, "Hey, how did you do with meeting our purpose today?"

Of course, really living into your purpose takes more than words; it takes action. The conversation is just where it starts, and it has to be consistent.

You also want to create opportunities for your family to experience your work environment. I realize that is easier for some people than others. (If you're working in a coal mine, you probably don't want to take your kids with you!) If you have an office, though, create situations where your kids can come in with you and learn something about what you do there. Don't make it uncomfortable, where kids aren't welcome or can't touch anything for fear of breaking it. If you are able to, make your work space comfortable for your family to come by and visit you.

And whenever they do visit, make them the stars. Don't make them feel like an inconvenience to you, even if you're on a phone call or in a meeting. Don't shame them for interrupting. Let them see or hear you talking with your customer or client and, if necessary, take a moment to tell them, "Hey, bud, I'm on the phone right now, and this conversation is going to help me love people through finances. We're talking about how Mr. Doe can align his investment portfolio with his values. I'll be off the phone in a few minutes and we can talk about whatever you want." Moments like this let you share your purpose and explain *why* what you're doing is so important, rather than just saying, "I'm on the phone."

My daughter Cambria and I went on a date at a coffee shop downstairs from my office the other morning. (More on weekly kid dates in the next chapter.) While we were there, I told her that I had to run upstairs to pick up a computer for the new house. She was happy to come with me, because she knows the office is a place where she's welcome and she's totally comfortable there. My employees are great about talking with her, and Cambria knows what happens in our office, so she connects well with them.

My work is invited into my purpose as well, and encouraging families to come in and feel comfortable is part of our company's culture. In our benefits section, it's clearly stated that, "Your kids are welcome here." And that's not just something we say. If someone brings their kids into work, they'll often find me down on the ground playing with them or challenging them to video games.

And if you want to see one of the most powerful results of inviting your family into your work purpose, my son told me that he wants to work for Stewardship when he grows up. The other kids in his class want to be in the NBA or to be firefighters or astronauts, but Parker wants to be like *me* when he grows up. I didn't tell him that's what he should do—or even that he *could* work at Stewardship—that's just what he wants because he's seen the impact we have.

One of my best friends, and a co-founder of Stewardship,

Brandon, has three kids who all feel the same way. His three boys are best buds with Parker, and they all fight about who gets to take which position after we die (nope, not retire)! That's how connected they are to our purpose, and how wonderful they believe it to be.

REBUTTALS

"My work purpose is just to get paid so I can have money."

Your work purpose is not about money; it's about what the money provides and what that can lead to. What do you want to do with that money? If you want to provide more for your family, well, guess what? That's your actual purpose. If you want to earn more money so you can donate more, that's your purpose.

I want to challenge you to get outside the mindset of money, because it's probably leading to the lack of harmony you experience in your life. Work is about so much more than just money.

Your work purpose is about making an impact on others, so start thinking about how you do that. Write notes in the section at the end of this chapter. Who is positively impacted by the work you do? How is their life made better by your work? Think this through all the way from micro-interactions to the bigger picture.

For example, at Stewardship one of the things we do is help people get home loans. How does that help, and who is impacted through that? First, we get to work with the vendors who help close that home loan. We build relationships with these folks and provide an income for them by having these transactions, and that impacts their lives in a positive way. And that's just on the vendor side!

Now let's talk about the customer. Not only do we provide them with a home loan, but we also provide them with a great interest rate at a great payment that is affordable within their budget. Now they have a cornerstone for their personal financial future. Beyond that, now they have a *home*, a place where they can sleep and make memories, where they will raise their families. That makes a huge positive impact on their lives. As a result of owning that home, their families are provided with a sense of security and safety. It becomes a positive place in the community, a productive dwelling in the neighborhood. You could even look at all the positive impacts on the entire neighborhood.

My work purpose is definitely more than just the paycheck I receive from helping people with home loans.

"I do have a purpose in my work, so much so that I pursue it like crazy. And the pursuit is why I don't have work–life harmony. All I want to do is pursue that work

purpose I'm passionate about, so I don't have time for my family or even for myself."

The reality is that you can't have harmony if you are over-worked. If you have too much work on your plate, this book can't help you. When you are overworked and have too many opportunities because your purpose is so great, the truth is that you will have to start saying no—no to work, no to clients—or you have to hire a team. (My first book just so happens to be a playbook for how to hire an effective team!)

If you feel like you're not in a position to hire a team but you still feel overwhelmed or overworked and you're yearning for work-life harmony, I have good news: we're going to discuss how to do that in forthcoming chapters.

"We've never done this before, so won't it seem weird to start talking with my family about purpose all of a sudden? Where do I even start?"

You start *somewhere*. It's never too late to create a purpose.

Here's a script you can start with and use your words to make it your own: "For too long I haven't communicated with you guys about what I do at work and the impact that's being made. And I want to tell you about it, not because I want to tell you how awesome I am, but because I want to start including you in it. When you love and support me, when you make me smile and give me energy and encouragement, I want you to know that your actions and the way you care for me help me work better. I want to start telling you how awesome *you* are and start letting you know that when you're awesome like that, it has a huge impact on people."

"My kids are too old. They are already in high school and college. I don't think they'll go along with this."

Your kids are never too old, and they will go along with it, because every human being is wired to want to make an impact on others. Every person is born to do something greater than themselves. Everyone wants to serve, care, and love in that way. You just have to invite them in.

This doesn't happen overnight, and it's not going to happen after just one conversation. My daughter was able to write a letter like the one I shared with you because I've invited my family into my work purpose and we've had many conversations about it.

You have to continually invite your family into your purpose, and I guarantee you that if you continue to invite them in over the years, no matter how old they are, whether they are two or twenty-two, they will have pride in you and in the work you're doing, and they will have pride in the way they support you and the role they play in your life.

"Grant, this sounds great but I doubt my parenting skills or ability to execute this."

I know, based on what you've just read, that it may sound like I have it all together or that I have unbelievable parenting skills, but the truth is I'm just a normal guy. This chapter includes some really cool highlights that I'm proud of, but I'm still a sinner who makes mistakes every day. My parenting isn't perfect. As you'll read later, in the "Evaluation" chapter, I'm constantly evaluating and trying to get better—and I've been on this journey for a long time.

So no matter how confident you are in your parenting skills, no matter where you're at in your relationship with your kids, both you *and your kids* deserve an effort. You deserve to get started on this journey and give it a shot. I promise you, with consistent, intentional actions—which I'm going to outline further in the remaining chapters—you too will have some amazing stories that you are proud of, in the same way I am of the stories I shared with you in this chapter.

(And as a matter of fact, when you do have those parenting wins, I would absolutely love for you to share those on social media and tag me in the post, because I want to celebrate with you when they happen!)

COMMUNITY

You may have started seeking work–life balance because you wanted a closer connection with your family—but that pursuit of balance only leads to more stress, guilt, and disconnect. With harmony, however, this purpose reconnects you with your family and then your family connects to the broader community that you all serve together.

The fundamental thing about harmony is that it doesn't exist with just one person. In a business, you have to have somebody to serve. In a family, you have someone else (or several other people) you are connected to. You cannot create harmony on your own. As a result, when you create work–life harmony, you are removing loneliness because there's no such thing as being alone and in harmony. Connecting your family and your work to your purpose creates community.

Before, the people you care about most had no idea about the impact you make on the world through your work. But now you're able to talk to your family about your work purpose so they understand and can support it. You can also talk to your family about your life purpose, and that support then creates community and connection.

When you have a family with a purpose that is selfless, others-focused, and that requires sacrifice, it brings people together. It will naturally create connections and closeness, a tight-knit family, more than you've ever had before.

If you want to test that, go on a mission trip together. Take your family to a homeless shelter and genuinely serve other people together. Watch what happens to your family: everybody will let go of themselves in that opportunity of service to genuinely make life about others in that moment. Your family will remember both the experience and the feeling for the rest of their lives.

If you want a tighter-knit family, you have to have a purpose that is about others. That purpose will bring you closer, make you more connected, and help you make beautiful harmony together.

KEY TAKEAWAYS

- Create a work purpose statement by answering four questions:
  - What is the purpose you're fulfilling every day?
  - Who are the people you are making an impact on?
  - What type of impact are you making on them?
  - How are you making their world a better place?
- Connect your work purpose to your family by having intentional conversations about the impact you make, how you change the world through what you do—and how your family is a part of that through their love and support for you.
- Invite your family into your purpose and live out that purpose through the intentional actions you take every day. Share your parenting wins on social media and tag me, @ GrantBotma on Twitter and Instagram, so I can celebrate with you!

MY INTENTIONAL ACTIONS

....

....

....

....

....

....

....

....

....

....

....

....

....

A QUICK WIN: THE MOST WONDERFUL
TIME OF THE YEAR

My family uses the Christmas holiday—a season of giving—as a time to really put our family purpose into action. We look at Christmas as an entire season for loving others.

It can be easy for kids to get caught up in the selfish aspects of Christmas, thinking about what they're going to get under the tree or only wanting to focus on the decorations and cookies and all the *stuff* that goes along with Christmas. We want to redirect that attitude because selfishness makes the holidays miserable.

So we purposely refocus the holidays to be about others. Because we have younger kids, we make it fun and gamify helping others for the holidays.

But you don't have to wait until the holidays to serve with your family.

As a family, think of someone in your life who is in need and how you can help serve them. Maybe they need something big like a bike, which you and your family can buy for them. Maybe they need something smaller, like a meal because they had a tough day, so you all work together to prepare something for them to enjoy. Maybe you know someone who could use more family time, so you buy them some board games or video games to play together.

Whatever they need, have your family go together to drop it off to that person—but try doing it in secret! Try "ding-dong ditching" them: placing the gifts on the families' front porches, knocking or ringing the doorbell, then running away and hiding so they can't see who left them these surprises. It's super fun, and kids love it.

When we do this, we drink hot chocolate and blast Christmas music super loud, and the kids sing along. They're always full of joy and excitement—and they're not thinking about themselves. It's exciting to be doing something fun and giving for these other people. They truly enjoy watching these other families get blessed, and they look forward to doing it every year. Oftentimes the families that we've blessed will go on to bless other families in future years, so it spreads.

And this is just one example of how our family's purpose of loving others is about finding ways to genuinely make life about others. The holidays aren't the only opportunity. We also serve at church together. My wife teaches the kindergarten-through-third-grade children's class, and my kids serve with her. Whenever our kids go to summer camp, I go with them to volunteer. We donate food and time to the food bank. They see us serving and loving others all year long. It's really about being the example and showing them what loving others looks like so that they can live out our purpose too.

CHAPTER 3

YOUR IDEAL YEAR

When I was just out of high school, my friends and I loved going to punk rock shows. Sometimes, at the smaller shows, we'd get to see or even hang out with the band afterward. We thought it was cool to grab their set list—the list of songs they played, in the order they planned them—to keep as a souvenir of the show. Usually this was just handwritten on a piece of paper, though bigger bands with larger productions would have their set list on a computer with a screen they could see from the stage.

No matter how it was written, a set list tells everybody in the band what they're going to do that night—what song they're going to open and close with, the breaks they'll take between sets, the different flow of energy throughout the whole show. Without those lists, the experience wouldn't be the same. First, the band members wouldn't all be on the same page. Additionally, they wouldn't be able to prepare for which song is coming next and who needs to play what. Finally, if they play all their hits right up front, the crowd is going to be dead for the rest of the set.

Instead, the band intentionally designs their ideal show, determining where to start and end, where they want higher-energy songs and where to slow it down a bit, where to sprinkle in the crowd favorites and where to try something new. By doing this work ahead of time, planning out the set list, everybody knows what to expect. And if, once they're playing, they decide to change something, the band has a quick chat, crosses out one song, and updates the set list, whether that's between shows or even between sets. They don't expect it to be perfect; there's always room to make adjustments.

COMMUNICATION

Now that you have created your purpose statement and invited your work and your family into that purpose, it's time to take that mindset piece of the previous two chapters and put it into action. But before I show you the practical application for that purposeful paradigm shift, we need to talk...about communication.

Communication is another necessary element of harmony.

Discord and tension occur when your family has no idea what's happening at work and your work has no idea what's happening at home. For example, if my wife thinks that I'll be home by five but I don't show up until six, she's going to be frustrated. She's been home all day with little kids, and she's been watching the clock, ready for a break. She may not have set the expectation that she wanted me home by five—but I also failed to set the expectation that I would be home at six.

Similarly, if my team expects me to arrive at nine every morning, but one day, without saying anything to anyone, I just don't show up until two in the afternoon—even if it's for a completely legit reason like a doctor's appointment—it's not going to lead to a harmonious environment.

These are day-to-day examples (and we'll look at those rhythms more in the next chapter), but this problem is only exacerbated on a larger scale—and then it can lead to even more serious problems.

If expectations aren't managed on an annual basis—for example, if your family has no idea when the busy seasons are for your work—it's difficult for them to keep going, to keep sacrificing and supporting you with no end in sight. Imagine if you asked your family to sing a note at the top of their lungs. They love you, so of course they'll do it if you really want them to. But if you don't tell them how long they have to sing, it will be hard for them. And then it will become hard for you, too, because at some point they're just not going to be able to sing anymore, and you'll become frustrated because you asked them to sing and they stopped. The problem here isn't that they stopped; it's that you didn't tell them how long to sing.

You can eliminate that problem, and get back on the path to work–life harmony, by managing expectations—and the best way to do *that* is by creating an ideal year calendar. The ideal year calendar helps set expectations on a big scale.

More than anything, this ideal year calendar is the number one conversation tool or trigger point to have a conversation with your family to let them know why you're going to be busy. "Hey, Daddy's going to be busy because I'm speaking at this event in the next couple of weeks, and this is an opportunity for me to love people through finances and share with them how we do things at Stewardship. That's thousands of people I get to share and talk with. I'll be really tired and it's going to take a lot of work, so I'm going to need your support during that time. But afterwards, we're going to celebrate together! We're going to celebrate on the beach! And on the way we can talk about all the people we're making an impact on."

This calendar, combined with effective communication, is

how you invite your family into your work, your work into your family—and both of those into your overall purpose.

Communication is going to look different for different families, for different people of different ages, and even for different seasons of life. But the principle of making the effort to communicate and manage expectations remains the same. When we don't communicate effectively, expectations go unmet. When we create our calendar, we're communicating what we want our life to look like. We're getting on the same page.

If my family or work team tries to sing the same song I'm singing but with a different beat, it's not going to sound good. But when we sing together, with the same beat, the same rhythm, the same tune—which we're all clear on because we've communicated it clearly before the concert—we make beautiful harmony.

CREATE AN IDEAL YEAR CALENDAR

The most powerful way to invite your family and your work into your life purpose is by creating what I call an ideal year calendar.

STEP 1: LIST YOUR ANNUAL PRIORITIES

The very first step is to list your priorities. These are things going on your calendar that you want to make sure to do every single year, no matter what. You may not do them exactly at the time you have them listed, but before the next twelve months are up, you will do these priorities every single time.

I have four categories to consider when creating my calendar:

- Marriage
- Parenting
- Work
- Rest/self-reflection

Within each of these categories, I have a priority for the year.

Marriage Priority: Anniversary Trip

Every year around our anniversary, my wife and I get away for at least one night. Depending on the year, it may be multiple nights. It might be something elaborate, like going to Mexico or the Bahamas, or it may be just staying at a local hotel. No matter what, though, we get away and celebrate the fact that we are married for another year. Along with celebrating another year of marriage, we also evaluate our marriage in a very intentional way. I will walk you through that step-by step-process in Chapter 6. For now, just know that prioritizing your marriage each year is a big deal.

Parenting Priority: Birthday Trips

Every year, I go on a one-on-one trip with each of my kids around their birthday. It's rarely on their actual birthday, but it's sometime around there. This trip is something super fun for each kid, so I budget for it to be a splurge, but the most important part is spending lots of quality time together. One of the best ways I've found to spend quality time with my kids is to travel with them, just the two of us, together. I try not to be on my phone, even if we're just sitting in silence, so we're truly in those moments together, even if that just means sitting next to one another, on an airplane, bus, Uber, or in the hotel. I put away work for a day or two so I can focus entirely on them.

One time, my son and I went to Chicago because we're big Cubs fans. We stayed at a hotel right across the street from Wrigley Field, went to a Cubs game on Friday night, then rented a car and drove to South Bend, Indiana, to see a Notre Dame game on Saturday. One of my daughters and I also went to Chicago, but we saw the musical *Matilda* and served together at a food bank. My other daughter and I drove to the beach in California and went to Legoland, just me and her. I give them options for these trips, but for the most part it's whatever they want to do, whatever really fun thing they're into at the time.

These trips were elaborate, but other years we've done things closer to home. One time we stayed in town and stayed for a night at the Cambria Hotel, because that's my daughter's name. We ate dinner at the Cheesecake Factory and ate a ton of pasta together. During the pandemic, travel was off the table, so all three of my kids chose to have a campout in the break room at my office. We brought a bunch of blankets and pillows to set up as a tent, watched movies on a projector, and just camped out instead of going to a hotel or on an adventure.

The point here is not how much money is spent. Don't let cost be the barrier for making stuff like this happen.

After a trip to Chicago with my son, I asked him, "Hey, Parker, what was your favorite part of the trip?" We got to stay at really nice hotels, eat great food, and experience his favorite sports teams with his favorite players. Anthony Rizzo, his favorite player, even handed him a ball. I expected him to say that was the coolest thing ever. But no. He responded, "Just being with you, Dad."

Work Priority: Annual Retreat

Every year, the other founders of Stewardship and I get away for a weekend retreat to review the previous year and create goals for the year to come. We try to create three big goals we want to accomplish before we get together again the following year.

During this retreat, we go over our budget and finances. We

dig through anonymous employee surveys, take personality tests, and share our results to learn more about ourselves and each other. It's a lot of deep, heavy work, and we also have fireside chats, hang out, relax, and talk about where we see the future of Stewardship and our lives, too. More than anything, it's a wonderful weekend for connection. We bring our spouses, so they also get to connect with each other.

Rest/Self-Reflection Priority: Time Off

I take two months off every year, typically one in March, when my family and I attend spring training games, and another in September, when we have extended vacation time on the beach.

This time off is more than just spending time with my family; it's also vital to my business and personal well-being (and this time is not completely unplugged). I try to schedule this time during the less busy seasons of my work. Then my family gets to see that their support during the busy time leads to this time when I turn things off to focus on them. (It's easier for people at work too, that I'm not disappearing when we're at our busiest!)

This is the time where I read (or listen to) all those books that I added to my wish list throughout the year but didn't have time for. Sometimes I take an online course or a certification I've been wanting to do. I do some personal and professional development, like going to a conference or an event. I gain perspective, I do research, and I also work on business projects. I execute at least one project during this time off, because I love doing it. It's fun, and I'm good at it. And because I'm removed from the day-to-day tasks at work, I'm able to work on these projects without getting distracted. It fuels so much growth and success in our business because I'm able to hyper-focus on one project and put everything else aside.

During the day, I'm resting and hanging out with my family. At night, I get to work with no distractions. Either way, I'm at my best.

This time "off" might be the most important time I take in my career. It leads to amazing breakthroughs and allows me the time and focus to work really hard on things that can be game changers for loving people through finances. I can come back from a month off with almost an entire project ready to execute—and then the people I work with see that I come back from this time off with something tangible, and they're really excited. This is where we've started different branches of our business or different marketing campaigns, different automations or customer journeys.

These are my priorities, the things that I will do every year. I put everything else on pause and focus on my marriage, my kids, my business partners, and some intentional time away from the day to day.

Your priorities may look similar to mine, or they may be completely different—and that's okay. Maybe you're going to take that trip to your parents' cabin every year for Christmas, or you want to make sure you go to the lake every year for the Fourth of July. That's great! Write down whatever your priorities are, the things that are so important to you that you're going to make sure you do them, without fail, every year.

STEP 2: PUT YOUR PRIORITIES ON YOUR CALENDAR FIRST

Get out a calendar and look at the next twelve months. Mark out the times in your work where you're really pursuing your purpose and you know you always have busy seasons.

I typically have three busy seasons, and I mark them off because I know that it's difficult to schedule my annual priorities during those busy times. I want to put everything else on pause during my annual priorities, and that's hard to do when I'm needed at work.

If you're not totally sure when your busy seasons will be, make your best guess. Sometimes busy seasons come when you don't expect it. But know that you will have at least one busy season, and try to block out that time on your calendar.

Then mark out time for your annual priorities—including some rest before and after each busy period.

This is an *ideal* year calendar, so it's flexible. You don't have to put in specific dates. For my birthday trip with Cambria, I mark that it will happen sometime in January. I don't have the dates or flights or anything booked yet, so I just keep it general.

My busy seasons are typically toward the beginning of the year, in the middle of the year, and toward the end of the year, so I highlight those. Then I take another section and highlight the marriage and parenting priorities that I'm not going to miss. Then I know I can't schedule something else during those times, because I know those priorities are happening at that time.

I do try to take those times off before or after a busy season. My wife and I usually take our anniversary trip before the busy season in the summer. We get that time together, which is good, because we know that I'm going to have to hit work pretty heavily after that. It's almost like I get to prepare for the upcoming busy season and my wife prepares with me. My wife gets creative during the busy season and brings food to the office so we can eat together.

After you've entered your busy seasons and priorities for your spouse and kids, add any other priorities you have.

That's when I add my founders' retreat and my time off for rest and self-reflection. We'll look more at the importance of rest, and how to fit more of it into your calendar, in Chapter 5.

I started out really simple, similar to the first steps here. My very first ideal year calendar just had a line for the busy seasons, a couple of priorities written down, and notes for some of the times I wanted for rest.

Then, as I evaluated and adjusted, my calendar evolved and I was able to improve it year after year. And that turned into the work–life harmony I have today.

STEP 3: MAKE ADJUSTMENTS

Make adjustments for anything that overlaps.

Again, this calendar is an *ideal* year. It is not a "set in stone, cannot ever change, Ten Commandments" year. As a result, adjustments *will* need to be made. So, start making them right away. Refining your calendar at the beginning of the year will give you permission to make additional adjustments as the year plays out.

Common adjustments you may need to make will be for any overlaps. An example is I typically take the founders' trip with my business partners near the date of my wedding anniversary, so I sometimes have to adjust when I take those trips—but, no matter what, both trips *will* happen.

Making these adjustments is also an excellent opportunity to keep the communication going between you, your family, and your work. Creating the ideal year calendar, and talking about how it could play out, is a wonderful way of setting expectations and inviting your work team and your family into this one life that you are living.

BONUS STEP

Identify bank or federal holidays that your employer observes. Write them into your calendar so you know in advance when those days are coming. Instead of letting those three-day weekends surprise you, intentionally plan in advance what to do with that free time off.

Here is an example of what my ideal year calendar has looked like at this stage:

ANNUAL SCHEDULE EXAMPLE

Here is an example of what my schedule may look like in a given year

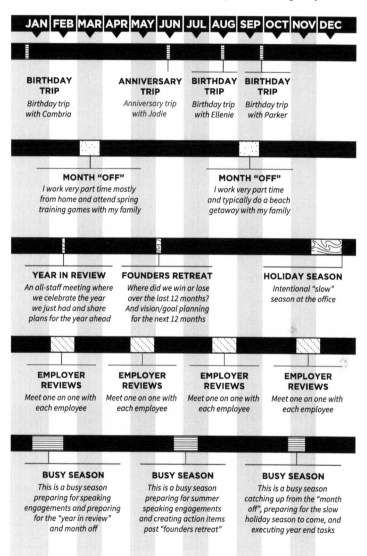

| JAN | FEB | MAR | APR | MAY | JUN | JUL | AUG | SEP | OCT | NOV | DEC |

BIRTHDAY TRIP
Birthday trip with Cambria

ANNIVERSARY TRIP
Anniversary trip with Jodie

BIRTHDAY TRIP
Birthday trip with Ellenie

BIRTHDAY TRIP
Birthday trip with Parker

MONTH "OFF"
I work very part time mostly from home and attend spring training games with my family

MONTH "OFF"
I work very part time and typically do a beach getaway with my family

YEAR IN REVIEW
An all-staff meeting where we celebrate the year we just had and share plans for the year ahead

FOUNDERS RETREAT
Where did we win or lose over the last 12 months? And vision/goal planning for the next 12 months

HOLIDAY SEASON
Intentional "slow" season at the office

EMPLOYER REVIEWS
Meet one on one with each employee

EMPLOYER REVIEWS
Meet one on one with each employee

EMPLOYER REVIEWS
Meet one on one with each employee

EMPLOYER REVIEWS
Meet one on one with each employee

BUSY SEASON
This is a busy season preparing for speaking engagements and preparing for the "year in review" and month off

BUSY SEASON
This is a busy season preparing for summer speaking engagements and creating action items post "founders retreat"

BUSY SEASON
This is a busy season catching up from the "month off", preparing for the slow holiday season to come, and executing year end tasks

CONTINUING THE CONVERSATION

Once you have your busy seasons, periods of rest, and your priorities mapped out on your calendar, share them with your family.

Show them the busy seasons and explain to your loved ones why those times are so busy and how you get to fulfill your work purpose during that time. Remind them how your work purpose supports your family's purpose. Ask for their help, patience, and grace. Let them know that you may have to work late or you might be less focused, and apologize in advance. Finally, make sure they understand that *they* are a part of this busy season, too. You couldn't do it without their love and support.

Also show your family members that you have scheduled time with each of them where they get to take center stage, and show them those times on the calendar.

Not only does my family know about all the busy seasons I have at work, but my office knows about what I'm doing at home. Everybody in our office shares our ideal years with each other, projecting everybody's calendar up on a screen. That helps us all feel seen and supported.

This is how you invite your loved ones in, showing that you're going to be intentional about pursuing your life purpose, family purpose, and work purpose together.

IDEAL, NOT PERFECTION

I'll be honest, when my family and I first started having these conversations about purposes and ideal years, it felt strange and weird. We had never done this before, and that new experience was kind of uncomfortable at first. You may have similar feelings or experience some tension or friction—and that's okay.

You may also be feeling overwhelmed, thinking that if you create this ideal year calendar, you'll be obligated to live it out to 100 percent perfection, or else it will be an exercise in failure. I want to make it clear right up front: *that will never happen.* Life happens, opportunities present themselves, and problems arise. Things will happen in your schedule that you will be unable to control, and that's to be expected. When things don't go as planned, try not to get discouraged.

I've never lived out 100 percent of my ideal year calendar, and that's totally okay too. If you can live out 70 percent of what you planned for your ideal year, that's a huge win. The key word here is *ideal.* You're designing what you *want* to have happen throughout the next twelve months, which is better than just drifting through them. This year is going to happen no matter what, so the ideal year calendar is a way to create some intentionality that fosters more work–life harmony.

But, again, this is something to aim for. It's a North Star. If you shoot for 100 percent and hit 70 percent—or even 60 percent or 50 percent—that's still way more than 0 percent! That's 50 or 70 percent more than you're doing intentionally now. So you can let it happen at 0 percent or you can let it happen at 70 percent.

Additionally, it's worth pointing out that this is also something that continually evolves. My ideal year never looks like what actually happens. And the first time I tried to create an ideal year, it looked almost *nothing* like what actually happened—or like how I schedule my year now. I've been doing this for years, so I've adjusted my ideal year, added to it, and removed from it.

It's not something that you figure out one time. You make it yours, make adjustments to it, and you get to redesign it every year.

REBUTTALS

"I don't know if I can take time for an anniversary or birthday trip. And I certainly can't take two months off!"

Do it on a weekend or just for one night. It doesn't have to be a month or even a week. My kids don't really like to be away from home for longer than a night or two. Figure out when there's a bank or federal holiday and take advantage of that built-in time off for a three-day weekend. Can you turn that three-day weekend into four or five days off?

You don't have to start with two months off; I certainly didn't start there. I worked my way up from trying to take a week off in March. The first year, I took five days off. The next year, I made it up to a week and added a long weekend in September. Then, I made a goal of taking off two weeks in March and a week in September. Finally, I tried the full month off. In fact, the first time I was able to take off two full months in the year was in 2019. Be reasonable. It's an evolution. This process takes time.

"I don't know what dates I'm going to do this."

Remember, this is an ideal year. It's a guideline, or a template to follow. It doesn't have to include exact, scheduled dates. I rarely know the exact dates for any of the things I'm doing when I map them out, so I just put them in the calendar around the time I know I'm going to do them. My daughter Cambria's birthday is Christmas Eve, so I know we're going to take her birthday trip sometime in January because December can get crazy with other stuff going on. I just mark her trip in January, and then I can schedule the specific dates later.

"I don't know when my busy season is."

You can make a guess if you're not sure exactly when your busy season or seasons will be. You can't have all busy seasons *and* fit in your other priorities. If you're always busy, find when you're busiest. The reality is that you can't work "pedal to the metal" all the time, twelve months a year—and if you are, you probably need to get a new job, start saying no to work, or change your priorities.

If your busy season is flexible, then you need flexibility in the other areas of your life too.

One of my employees is like that. His busy seasons always change. So that means when he's creating his rest time, he needs to have a low barrier to entry (which you'll see in Chapter 5). When a busy season ends, he takes advantage of that preplanned pocketed downtime to get some rest.

"Grant, this sounds great, but I'm having a hard time getting my spouse or kids interested in doing this with me."

There are two reasons why they may not want to do this with you: one, you are having a hard time connecting with them; or two, you hurt them.

If you have hurt your family, the answer is easy: apologize, move forward, and keep apologizing!

But if you are having a hard time with connection, you'll

need to do more. First, look at what they are interested in. It's not about taking a trip or doing something really fun for *you*; it's about meeting them where they are, and doing what they're interested in. If you have a kid who's really into video games, maybe you can find a video game arcade or go to a video game tournament with them. Or you can just start playing video games with them. You can even just sit there and watch while they're playing video games, and give compliments when they do something cool.

You'll find that these kinds of conversations are so much easier when your family is already in a happy, fun place, when you've done something they care about and you're paying attention to them. So then when you do want to talk specifically about purpose, it doesn't feel so hard. You're making everybody feel excited about it.

This is all about meeting your loved ones where they are and inviting them into this conversation. It's not about you; you're inviting them into a purpose that's greater than you.

"Hey Grant, I have three kids too, and I don't have the money to take each of them on their own trip to Legoland."

That's fine. Don't take them to Legoland. Maybe you make them a great meal or go indoor camping in your living room. Use your imagination. There are ways to meet your kids or spouse where they're at without going over the top. It doesn't have to be expensive; it just has to happen.

All of your priorities should be easy and straightforward enough that you can do them every year, no matter what. The things you do might change from year to year, depending on what makes the most sense for your current situation. But it doesn't have to cost anything, other than the time spent; you get a return on that time in the form of memories made.

"How do I make this ideal year come to life? How do I live it?"

You live it by doing it! You make your priorities—well, a priority! There are also some daily, weekly, and quarterly rhythms and efficiencies you can make that help your year come to life too, which we'll discuss shortly.

NOT A ONE-MAN BAND

When you set people's expectations in this way, on a big scale with the ideal year, it makes it easier to use the same concepts to set their expectations on a week-to-week or day-to-day basis. Then you—and your team and loved ones—will see that these are not just words on the calendar; they're part of your life.

You need those important people in your life to be bought-in because it is impossible to pursue work–life harmony on your own. That's like trying to be a complete one-man band singing into a microphone, with a harmonica strapped to a cymbal strapped to a drum strapped to a trumpet, which is also strapped to a guitar.

Instead, maybe you're playing lead guitar, your family sings, and your work plays the drums—but you all play the same song, in the same key, and at the same tempo. You work together to come up with your set list and order of songs, to include everyone's ideas and maximize each person's talents, all of which makes the show even better.

You can't make harmony on your own; you need another sound. When you're singing the melody, it's beautiful. But when someone else comes in and supports the melody, that's called harmony—and those additional voices make the song even sweeter.

KEY TAKEAWAYS

- Consider your annual priorities—the things you want to make sure to do every single year, no matter what—and put those on your calendar first.

- Block off your busy seasons, time for rest before and after those busy seasons, and make any necessary adjustments so there's no overlap with your busiest times of year and your annual priorities.

- Continue to invite your family and your work into your purpose by sharing your calendar with them so they know what to expect and you are all on the same page.

- BONUS: If you'd like to see a video walk-through of how I create my ideal year calendar, please check out https://www. grantbotma.com/calendar.

MY INTENTIONAL ACTIONS

....

....

....

....

....

....

....

....

....

....

....

....

A QUICK WIN: TIME TO COME HOME

Every day, before you leave for work, let your family know what time you plan to be home. They have things going on in their days too, and giving them this information helps them plan accordingly.

Some pro tips:

1. You have to be a person of integrity. Your family has to trust that you'll do what you say—and if they don't believe that you'll be home when you say you will, you're going to have a really hard time implementing everything else.
2. Give yourself a little bit of a margin. If you think you'll actually be home at 5:15, tell your family 5:30, just in case something goes long, you get caught up doing one more thing, or you get stuck in traffic.
3. On days when you have some flexibility—for example, if you have appointments you can move around or you can leave the office early—ask, "What time would you like me home?" That allows your family to speak into your life a little bit, allowing you to serve instead of dictate. You may not be able to do that every day, but it makes a difference on the days you can. Use that to your advantage.
4. If things come up and that time changes, be sure to communicate that, whether through a phone conversation or something as simple as sending a text. This happens to me at least one day a week, so I always give my wife a

heads-up as soon as I know. And I manage these expectations whether I'm coming home later or earlier because she's making plans with her day and the kids based on what I communicated to her earlier.

CHAPTER 4

QUARTERLY, WEEKLY, AND DAILY RHYTHMS

It's hard to have harmony without rhythm. You could be singing the right tunes. You could have every part of the band in the right tune, but if you aren't in rhythm, without the proper timing, there's no harmony. There is no unity.

Rhythm makes music easier to follow along. Rhythms essentially keep everyone on track, on the same page. Despite how important rhythm is, it's often so seamless you might not even notice it—unless it's missing.

RHYTHMS OF LIFE

As with music, if we're seeking harmony in our life, we need to have rhythms.

Rhythms are important in daily life because they help us do the important things we all need to do intentionally and often. For example, if you want to drink more water, you might set an alarm reminding you to drink every hour—that's a rhythm. Or you may want to work out more. Just deciding to work out three times a week isn't enough to establish a rhythm, though. A rhythm would be setting a schedule to work out at a specific time every Monday, Wednesday, and Friday. Yes, the three times a week are built in, but by adding specific days and times, you actually create the rhythm and make it come to life.

What are the things in your life that matter, that are important to you? What do you need to do to help make your purpose come to life? Create rhythms for those things you need to make a priority, in order for you to be at your best to make your purpose come to life.

What's more, if something doesn't help bring your purpose to life, it *shouldn't* be a rhythm. There are already unintentional rhythms built into your day, like taking out your phone and browsing social media when you have idle time. But if you are intentional about when you do things—and yes, of course there's time to go on social media—you don't let your time drift away from you. I'm not saying don't do them; I'm saying to be intentional about how and when you do them, to help make your purpose come to life better.

When you create rhythms of things you do on a consistent basis, you can communicate them to your family and work, which can serve as a way of inviting others into your purpose. These rhythms also point to your purpose. So if my purpose is to love them, my family purpose is to love others, and my work purpose is to love people through finances, then all of my rhythms should help me better pursue these purposes.

As you will see, many of these rhythms involve somebody else, and that's intentional because it creates community and removes that sense of loneliness and isolation you may have felt before reconnecting with harmony. It's hard to feel all alone if you are intentionally celebrating time with your spouse and kids. Creating these rhythms also generates opportunities for better relationships and more connections to occur. It's important that my family feels that I care about them and make them a priority. If I'm not making my kids and my wife a priority, they're not going to want to be invited into my purpose. (Just like if I'm not also making people at work a priority, they won't want to be invited into anything I'm trying to do either!)

I'm going to share several examples of the rhythms I have set up in my life, but the rhythms of your life are likely going to be different—and that's okay.

Finally, it's not a rhythm if it's not repeated. Rhythms can happen daily, throughout the week, or even quarterly. In the last chapter, we talked about annual priorities. Now, we're going to look at the daily, weekly, and quarterly rhythms that further support those priorities.

PUT IT ON YOUR CALENDAR

You already started blocking out certain seasons and your annual priorities on your calendar in the previous chapter. Now, I want you to keep breaking down your rhythms in smaller and smaller pieces, from quarterly to weekly to daily, and put those on your calendar, too.

Everybody has these types of rhythms in their life; now, it's time for you to identify what you need to repeat on a quarterly, weekly, and daily basis to make that ideal year calendar come to life so you can meet your purpose. When you pay attention to your rhythms, you take control instead of letting time just happen to you—and potentially pass you by.

Keep these rhythms as easy as possible, so that they actually happen.

Make sure they help you meet your purpose. Don't do it just because you read it here. This isn't just one more check-list item or something to make you feel ashamed because you're not already doing it.

QUARTERLY RHYTHMS

Identify the important things for you to do each quarter, in all areas of your life. For example, what needs to happen at work—that only you can do—so that your workplace will be able to make the same impact on the world, and your purpose will be met?

In his book *Clockwork*, Mike Michalowicz calls this the "Queen Bee role." As the queen bee, there's something you have to do in order for everyone else in the hive to thrive. Identify your queen bee role—or, to relate it back to harmony, the things only *you*, as the lead singer, can do.

Two examples of this, for me, are creating content and developing my staff. If I'm not doing those two things every quarter, we're not going to be able to grow and innovate. When I do, however, we are better positioned to meet our purpose of loving people through finances.

Some of my quarterly rhythms include:

· **Development and education.** I'm never going to be perfect or have it all together. I have to keep working to improve myself. So every quarter, I create a rhythm to gain knowledge and information. This may mean going to a conference or an event related to work or church. It may mean reading something intentional about a specific industry I'm in.

- **Content planning.** My work purpose is to love people through finances, and one of the best ways I can do that is to educate them, which I do through content like podcasts, blogs, and videos. I create a quarterly rhythm to plan out the content I want to create, looking at what topics are relevant to our team and to society. This starts with a quarterly content meeting with my team, where we figure out what we want the podcast episodes, blog posts, and videos to be about. Having a plan allows us to better execute the content; otherwise, we'd show up every day and wonder what to do next.

- **Content creation.** Another quarterly rhythm I have, after our content planning meeting, is to batch create some of the content for the quarter. I'll record a lot of podcast episodes in just a few days—or even one day—which allows me to get the content done while I'm focused on just that one thing.

- **Meet with employees.** I meet with each of my employees one-on-one every quarter. Just like I want my wife and kids to know that I care about them, I also want my employees to know I care about them. If employees answer yes to the question, "Does my boss or supervisor care about me?" you're doing something right as a business leader. I ask them how we're doing with our mission or purpose of loving people through finances, and what we could be doing better or differently.

- **Professional development.** I also have quarterly meetings with my admin staff. We use these meetings as opportunities to grow and get better with a new endeavor, training, or tool. Then I separately do something similar with my sales staff, because they are two different roles.

WEEKLY RHYTHMS

After you have your quarterly rhythms listed out, look at what you need to do weekly in order to meet your purpose and be in the best shape possible—mentally, physically, and spiritually.

My weekly rhythms include:

- **Weekly date with my wife.** This is important because my wife is my best friend and biggest supporter. She and I have a strong desire to spend time together. She keeps me in check, making sure I don't get too prideful or arrogant. And she thinks differently than I do, so she helps me see things from other perspectives or talk them through in different ways. Because she helps me love people better, I need to spend time with her, so I have to actually make that happen. I might have the best of intentions to be a husband who spends time with his wife, but I have to follow that up with an intentional action.
- **Coffee dates with my kids.** Another weekly rhythm I have is doing a weekly coffee date with one of my kids

each week, on a rotating basis. I like coffee, and my kids all like vanilla steamed milk or a pastry from the coffee shop. It feels like a treat for them—both getting a treat to eat or drink and getting to do something different. Sometimes we just sit together and don't talk about much. When I went on a coffee date with my younger daughter, Ellenie, this past week, I asked her, "How am I doing as a dad? Am I being a good daddy right now?" She told me, "You're doing great, Dad." And that was it. We just enjoyed our time together. Other times, we'll need to have conversations about something my wife and I have seen, like exhibiting a selfish attitude, or I'll console them about something that has happened in their lives. All too often life can just pass us by, and we think, "I need to have this conversation with my spouse or my kids," but we don't make the time to ensure that those conversations happen.

- **Working out.** I do my best to work out three days a week on a set schedule.
- **Rest.** I have a rest rhythm to my week, which typically includes a day of rest all day on Sundays.
- **Work review.** Every week, I review the previous week to see what went on and how productive I was over that week. I try to determine how well I did, what worked, and what didn't work, to see where I can improve. I also look to the week ahead to see what I need to prepare for the week. Finally, I create my "Big Three" for the week: every week, I have three big things I want to accomplish

in order to consider the week a success. I look back to see if I accomplished my Big Three last week and if not, what prevented me from doing so. If I did, I look at what helped get me there and make sure that the next Big Three are challenging enough and that they help me meet my purpose of loving people.

· **Monday meetings.** I like to do what I call Meeting Mondays, where everybody on my team knows that Mondays are for meetings. We do as many of our meetings as we can on one day, which allows us to keep a mindset of collaboration instead of feeling like those meetings are encroaching on our ability to get other stuff done throughout the week.

Because these rhythms happen weekly, try not to make them too elaborate. My wife and I don't go out to an expensive restaurant for steak and lobster every week, and we don't go on vacation every weekend. Sometimes we just grab coffee and talk. Sometimes we walk around our neighborhood at sunset or sit on our porch. The bottom line is just figuring out ways to spend time with each other and to focus on each other—not what we eat or where we go.

Keeping it simple allows for these rhythms to actually happen. When I take my kids to a coffee shop, it's not expensive or elaborate. It doesn't require effort or planning.

DAILY RHYTHMS

We talked earlier about managing other people's expectations, but sometimes you need to manage your own expectations as well, and that's where your daily rhythms come into play.

It's easy for days to get away from us, ending up full of busy work and inundated with meetings, leaving us feeling like we're struggling to get through the day-to-day. But by setting up some rhythms and routines, you can manage your expectations and execute your day to better serve your purpose.

My daily rhythms include:

- **Start up.** I also have a daily startup rhythm when I start work, where I create my Big Three for the day (a concept I got from Michael Hyatt). Those daily Big Threes help me work toward accomplishing my weekly Big Three. I look at my schedule for the day, see what I have going on, prepare mentally, and make sure I can accomplish my weekly Big Three. I ask myself, "What am I going to do today, to make that happen?"
- **Phone.** Another daily rhythm I have is putting my phone away when I come home from work, so that I'm present at dinner with my wife and kids. Having that rhythm in my day also helps me stop working and shift my focus to my family.

- **Sleep.** I'm a big believer in sleep. My body needs it more than food or water; you can die faster without sleep than you will without food or water.[4] I do take a day of rest on Sundays, and I sleep a lot that day, but I try to make sure to get plenty of sleep every day throughout the week, as well. To do this, I create intentional time for it.

As a starting point, think of three rhythms for each—three quarterly rhythms, three weekly rhythms, and three daily rhythms—that you can commit to.

If that sounds overwhelming right now, let's look at some ways you can be more efficient, so you get back some time in your busy life and actually make these rhythms happen.

BE EFFICIENT

People often ask me how I manage to be a business owner, an author, and present for my family. In other words, how do I actually make all of these rhythms happen? The answer is that I have to be very intentional with my time and as efficient as possible, to make my purpose come to life.

Efficiency means using your time *intentionally*. Making choices takes energy, and choosing the things you are going to do can be a barrier to actually *doing* those things. If you're efficient, you can make the choices ahead of time and then

4   https://hbr.org/2011/03/sleep-is-more-important-than-f

repeat the choices that have worked previously. Efficiency also removes decision fatigue, the mental energy you have to spend making decisions. It's about decreasing that fatigue while still doing the things you need and want to do.

You can also make intentional choices in different areas of your life to save time. When people think they need work-life balance, what they're actually thinking is, "I don't have enough *time*."

I don't have a magic solution to give you more time, but I can help you make better use of the time you do have— without taking time away from any of the important areas of your life. You already know I'm not going to tell you to work less, to take time away from that pursuit and use it differently. Instead, I'm going to show you how being more efficient means that you can get more done in less time so you can better live out your purpose.

One example of how I use my time efficiently is on my commute. When I'm driving, I typically (and intentionally) do one of three things:

- About 80 percent of the time, I gain knowledge by listening to a podcast, audiobook, or sermon.
- I sit in silence and pray about 10 percent of the time.
- I have fun 10 percent of the time. I blast the stereo as loud as I can and belt out a good song.

Instead of spending my drive home worrying about work, listening to opinions on talk radio, or mindlessly driving, I'm using that time to intentionally do something that matters to me. I'm not wasting that time. It's time that I have to spend driving, so I'm using it for something, instead of taking time away from my wife or kids or work. That's time I can use.

I'm also efficient with my vacations. Whenever I need some time with my family, or just emerged from a busy season and need time to rest away from home, we have some go-to spots we like as a family. For us, it's the beach in Carlsbad, California. It's comfortable for us, and close to Legoland, where my kids like to go. We can drive there, which means we don't have to worry about plane tickets or travel. There's a very low barrier to entry—it doesn't require a lot of thinking and there's not much standing in the way of making it happen. If we wanted to go tomorrow, we could get in the car and get away.

Having efficient vacation choices in your pocket is super helpful, particularly because vacations are a different form of rest that can help you rest more efficiently. They don't have to be elaborate, expensive, or mind-blowing places. Sure, sometimes you want to go to Hawaii or Fiji, and don't rule that out. Just be intentional about when you want to go on big, blowout trips, and when you simply want to get away for a period of rest to somewhere comfortable and familiar that doesn't require you to figure out where to go or how to get there. You can switch into rest mode even faster.

My wardrobe is another area where I'm very efficient. I don't go full-on Mark Zuckerberg or Steve Jobs, but I'm close. I basically wear the same style of jeans (or shorts, depending on the weather) and the same shirt in a few different colors. That works for me because I don't have to go through my wardrobe every day and figure out what to wear. I just grab something, know it matches, and I'm ready to hit the day, do the work I need to do, and focus on my purpose.

I spend less than two minutes getting dressed each day, whereas most people are spending up to ten. That adds up over a week—and even more over a month, year, or a lifetime!

Let's say it takes you seven minutes every morning to choose your clothes and get dressed. It takes me two. That means I save five minutes every day, which adds up to 1,825 minutes saved every year—or more than thirty hours! *More than one whole day!* And that's just one choice. Imagine how much time you can use when you add up all of your efficient choices. If you make five efficient choices and they each save you the same amount of time, you get more than six days back at the end of the year. Now you can build up how much time you take off or use those bonus days to pursue your purpose.

And if you don't want to wear the same shirt every day, there are other ways to be efficient—try a capsule wardrobe, where everything is mix and match—or you can choose a different area to focus on.

I'm also efficient with my meals, because I don't choose what to eat. My wife and assistant make those decisions for me. My wife cooks at home, and my assistant orders my lunch so I can just work until food shows up at my office door. I have created a list of foods I like and presented to her ahead of time, but I don't have to choose. I also don't spend time having conversations about where to go to lunch, who's going to drive, or what to order.

Sometimes, though, you may want to use that lunch hour as a rhythm of rest for you. I do that from time to time. Other times, I engage in conversations. On those days, I ask my assistant not to order lunch so I can go eat with someone in the office. But I only do that intentionally, when I'm making the choice to do so and it seems like a good use of my time, not by default.

My weekly dates are another area of efficiency. My kids and I have two coffee shops that we choose from. And my wife and I have a small handful of places we like to go for our dates. We don't spend time wondering where to go; we show up, execute, and use that time actually being together.

I choose specific times throughout the day to check email or use social media. I try to only check my email twice a day, and I intentionally schedule it because otherwise that time can slip away very quickly. Rather than having the screen steal my time, I choose when I'm going to engage with the screen.

You could choose to batch things, too. I batch-create content, but maybe you can batch-cook a bunch of meals and have them ready to go for the week. My friend Amy Porterfield of the *Marketing Made Easy* podcast has an awesome episode all about doing batch work. It is episode #182, "How to Mega-Batch Your Content." I strongly recommend checking that out at https://www.amyporterfield. com/2017/10/182-how-to-mega-batch-your-content/.

These are examples from my life, and I'm not saying that you have to be efficient in the same ways or areas I am. If you care about what you wear every day or what and where you eat for lunch, that's okay. You probably won't make the same efficiency choices I do in those areas, but you can find other areas that don't matter as much to you, where you can remove some of the decision time and decision fatigue.

You also don't have to start with all of these at once. Just pick one and do it for a month straight. Then choose another one and add that. Eventually, these efficient habits build up and you hardly notice the change—but you'll definitely notice how much time you've saved!

LIFE HACKS

There are simple hacks you can do to be as efficient as possible. These may include:

- Putting your bills on autopay
- Enrolling in direct deposit
- Setting up recurring deliveries for things you buy consistently
- Getting a robot vacuum for your house, so you don't have to do it yourself
- Signing up for subscription meal boxes so you don't have to think about what's for dinner
- Scheduling someone to come to your house or office to do oil changes, wash your car, and/or groom your pets

These hacks save time, but they also save a lot of mental energy.

Additionally, you can set up triggers in your day that activate certain efficiencies or rhythms. For example, if you want to make sure to be home by a certain time, you can schedule an alarm on your computer or phone that plays Loverboy's "Working for the Weekend" as loud as possible. When you hear that song, you know it means it's time to get out of there—and it makes it harder to have another conversation or write one more email.

REBUTTALS

"I can't do that!"

Again, these are ideal rhythms. Things shift, evolve, and change. Although my team and I plan out our content every quarter, some of what we intend to post changes. If we need to make an adjustment, that's totally fine. My wife and I try to go on a date every week, but do we make it happen every single week? No, of course not. Life gets in the way, and we're not perfect at any of these rhythms. Don't expect 100 percent perfection. Again, if you can get to 70 percent, you're doing amazingly well.

"I can't think of a different place to go on date night every week; I just don't have that kind of creativity."

This may be the number one reason why people I know don't date their kids or their spouse. But, as I mentioned in this chapter, you don't need to be creative or come up with something new all the time! Just pick one place that everybody likes and do that. Find a coffee shop or a diner or a park and go there every time. You could even make a list of places and allow your child or wife to pick from that list. Make that decision once instead of having to make it every week. Make sure it's in the calendar too, and then all you have to do is show up.

"Don't your wife and kids get sick of going to the same place?"

Not really. But if they do, we can change where we go; that's fine. I'm sure they'll want to go somewhere different when they're sixteen than they do when they're six. I'm not saying to never be creative or that you're stuck for life; I'm just saying not to make this a hard decision. Just like I usually wear the same thing every day, but I don't wear those jeans and shirt if I'm going to a wedding. I bust out a suit from the corner of my closet.

It's not about where you're going or what you're wearing; it's about having time to pursue your purpose. I go on dates with my wife and my kids so they know I care about them; it's not important which coffee shop we go to.

"Doesn't that get boring? Don't you ever want to be spontaneous?"

For me, no, it doesn't get boring, and I leave room for spontaneity. You can be efficient and have fun too. I do go on elaborate dates with my wife or on elaborate vacations sometimes. I just don't do that all the time.

Journey sings the same greatest hits at every concert, and they still sell out every time. There's value in nostalgia. One of the reasons why music is so powerful is because it evokes memories. Some of these efficiencies can do the same thing. Going back to the same vacation spot creates cool memories, which leads to nostalgia. If you remember what a great time you had last time, you're probably going to be eager to go and have a great time again.

If Journey does it, so can you. Don't stop believing.

KEY TAKEAWAYS

- Determine three quarterly, weekly, and daily rhythms you can stick to—and get them on your calendar!
- Choose one area where you can commit to being more efficient for the next month, so you have more time to focus on the priorities and rhythms that help you live out your purpose.
- If you have other tips and tricks to be more efficient, I'd love to hear them! Send them to me on social media, @ GrantBotma. You may think it's no big deal or that everybody knows that, but your tip or trick could potentially help another person save time and energy to pursue their purpose!

MY INTENTIONAL ACTIONS

....

....

....

....

....

....

....

....

....

....

....

....

....

A QUICK WIN: YOUR GO-TO VACATION

Sometimes you need to celebrate or you want to have a little respite or getaway with your family. It's easier to execute those things with your ideal year and rhythms if you have some ideas for go-to places in your pocket.

My family and I love to go to a Mexican restaurant by our house, so that's a great, easy place for us to go for celebrations. Sometimes we'll take the kids to the Cheesecake Factory as a special treat. There's also an ice cream place we absolutely love. Those are special places for us.

When it comes to vacations, we know that we always enjoy going to Carlsbad, California. If we need to get away, we can just jump in the car and go, making that vacation happen with very little planning.

Create a list of a handful of things you and your family like to do or places to go if you need something to do together. Where can you go to celebrate? To rest? Write it out or have it on your phone. Do the work ahead of time, then when the opportunity arises or it's time to do one of those things, if you need to execute some piece of your ideal year or rhythms, you can always do that.

1. Think of one place everybody in your family loves to go out to eat together.

2. Think of one inexpensive, simple place you can do a stay-cation with your family, whether that's a hotel or vacation rental nearby, or just an activity in your own town that you all enjoy.

3. Think of another place, a different city or state (but not necessarily requiring a plane flight), you can go for a mini vacation.

CHAPTER 5

REST

If all you do is sing at the top of your lungs for every second of a song, you might be able to get through the song, but you're not going to be able to do that again for another song right after, so that's going to be a pretty short concert.

My wife and I have a guilty pleasure of going to Las Vegas to attend concerts of outdated and aging stars. A few years ago, we went to a Britney Spears concert (don't judge us!), and it was probably one of the most entertaining evenings we've ever had. The show itself was extremely fun and unique, and there was also some great people-watching to be had.

Imagine, though, if during that concert Britney had to stop and say, "Hold on, guys. I'm really tired. I just need to rest for a moment." That would be so weird and awkward!

Instead, very intentional moments of rest are inserted in her songs and between each song. Sometimes Britney goes backstage while the dancers are doing their thing or they play a video on the giant screens. That didn't take away from the experience; we all enjoyed the show, and she got her rest.

The best lead singers intentionally build in time to rest their voices within a song. That's when the chorus or instrumental breaks occur.

A band going on tour doesn't perform every single day. They have to have weeks or months off from touring so they can rest—rest their vocal cords or fingers so they can perform at their best, and also rest their brains so their creativity can spark to write new songs or albums.

TIME TO REST

You can't have harmony if you're overworked and feeling overwhelmed. This book can't stop you from overworking; that's not what I'm trying to do.

Instead, we're going to talk about rest. Resting can help you recover from feeling overworked. If you're in that place now, where you are overworked and overwhelmed, you likely aren't getting proper rest as part of your rhythms.

One of my best friends—we played college basketball

together, his wife is great friends with my wife, our kids are homeschooled together, we're business partners, we do *life* together—was having a hard time resting. I told him that he needed to stop and get away, so I paid for him and his wife to go to one of my favorite hotels in California. At first he was a little reluctant, but his wife was so appreciative and excited that he went along with it.

To make a long story short, he crashed upon arrival—and ended up sleeping most of four days in a row. He'd wake up, eat, and go back to sleep. He physically crashed because he hadn't rested intentionally. And because he was just *done*, he and his wife didn't get to enjoy that vacation as much as they would have had he been resting all along.

This chapter is going to help you avoid that kind of burnout by teaching you to be proactive about planning for your rest. Don't just drift through your life hoping to get some rest someday (and suffer the consequences when you don't); intentionally design your life to include rest in it.

When you rest, you are able to deal better with busy seasons—and you can even thrive in the midst of them. Because I rest consistently, I get excited and start to look forward to those busy times. I think it's fun to work! And it's an act of worship, because I was created to contribute. But I wouldn't enjoy it—or be as good at what I do—without rest.

When I do the ideal year calendar with my team, the number one piece of positive feedback I get from my employees, my partners, and their spouses is my emphasis on how important it is to intentionally plan for rest before or after the busy season. When you are rested, you can handle those busy times better. And you know that they have an end to them—it won't *always* be busy—and then you can take another period of rest.

Invite your family into your rhythms of rest, too. My wife knows that we'll get rest after the busy season, or that we just had rest time as a family beforehand so we're both energized and ready. But before I became more intentional about my schedule, it felt like that busy season was going to go on forever, and that is unsustainable. At some point, you *and your family* have to stop and take a breath. Knowing you have a rest coming up means that you can push through until that intentional time built into the song for you to rest and breathe.

Even if it seems counterintuitive, when you rest you are able to be more productive, so you get sustainable growth in so many different areas of your life. I am a better husband, father, and leader at work when I rest.

Now, when I say rest, I'm not talking about sitting in solitude, doing nothing. It doesn't necessarily mean taking a nap. It's not sitting cross-legged with your shoes off and chanting a mantra. Rest doesn't even mean saying no to technology!

In fact, rest looks different for everyone, and everyone rests differently. Sometimes I rest by sitting on the couch watching a baseball game. I love it. Sometimes rest means taking a nap or getting some extra sleep. And sometimes I rest by doing projects around the house. I am energized when I see progress in something I'm building. After sitting at a desk, writing content or creating videos or holding meetings, it's nice to work with my hands.

At Stewardship, we produce live events for our clients and our community. I recently spoke at one of those events three nights in a row, and the first thing I did when I got home was start drilling and hammering to hang shelves so I could organize my garage—and that felt like rest! I was doing something different, breaking a sweat instead of speaking and poring over information, and that gave me the release I needed.

PLAN TO REST

You have to plan for your rest just like you plan everything else in your schedule, or it won't happen. You can't just get to Sunday and hope you get a day of rest; you have to intentionally make it happen.

Just as there are many different types of music, there are also different types of rest. Here are some ways to include rest in your day, week, quarter, and year.

DAILY REST

To make sure I have time for rest on a daily basis, I am very intentional with my schedule. And although I try to schedule as much of my day as possible, I have found that it's unwise to schedule 100 percent of my day with back-to-back tasks or appointments. That is too taxing and leaves no room for flexibility or rest.

The best way to naturally build rest into your day is by scheduling only 70 percent of your time. This allows for rest, and it allows for life to happen. If you still have more time in your day, you can work more than that, but if something comes up and you only hit that 70 percent, it won't lead to overwhelm. Things come up all the time, so leaving space for rest will let you work at your best. Scheduling 100 percent of your time is not sustainable over the long term.

Additionally, the break room in my office is a free environment that is conducive to different ways to rest. We have a projector screen and video game system. It's okay to intentionally rest while you're working and watch a YouTube video or an episode of your favorite show.

Of course, the number one form of rest that has to happen on a daily basis is sleep. Without sleep, you're going to struggle. Various studies have shown that lack of rest or sleep is one of the causes of cancer, both in terms of developing in the first place or growing more quickly. Any time you have an illness, doctors prescribe more rest, and that's for good reason. You need to sleep, and you have to be intentional about it. Six hours a day is fine, but in an ideal world you get at least eight hours, every day.

If you're thinking, "Sleeping eight hours is lazy," then you're calling me very lazy, because I sleep eight hours almost every day. Sleeping and resting is not being lazy, especially if you schedule it so you're intentional about it. That whole rise-and-grind mentality is a fool's errand. You might be able to get through your days, but you're sure not going to be giving your best effort for long.

It's not only okay to rest and sleep, it's wise to get as much sleep as you need. I rarely wake up earlier than seven thirty in the morning, and I often wake up later than that. I sleep a lot, and that's *good*.

WEEKLY REST

Do not discount the value of resting with the people you love most—but at the same time, don't feel guilty if you aren't able to rest with them every day. I don't get rest time with my wife or children every single day. I can't honestly tell you that my wife and I hold hands together in bed, look each other in the eye, and have deep, connective, restful moments every night. It just doesn't happen. Sometimes, the only time we get to connect in a day is in passing, while

I'm in the shower and she's brushing her teeth and we're both yelling over the sound of the water. And that's okay. It's not realistic to put that pressure on yourself, to both rest without others and with your family every day.

That's why we have those dates set up as weekly rhythms. Bonus: they count here as rest, too! A weekly date with your spouse or kid is you letting them know you care about them, as we previously discussed, but it's also you resting together. Sometimes that rest looks like going out to eat or to a coffee shop, but other times it might be playing laser tag, going to a movie, or going to the beach. This weekly time allows you to connect with them, talk with them, and just *be* with them.

The best value I've received in resting in my life has come from intentionally having a Sabbath day, a day focused on rest, every single week. When my family and I started doing that every week, it was a game changer. Intentionally creating a day where you don't do anything but rest together is beautiful.

But honestly? When we first started trying to do our rest day, we failed. We really struggled to figure out when to do it and, really, just *how* to do it. Sunday seemed like the most logical day, but then we ended up doing chores around the house or going different places, and we didn't feel very unified. We became successful at having an intentional day of rest when we figured out *we had to prepare for it the day before.*

If Sunday is going to be our rest day this week—and usually it is for us, though sometimes we pick a Friday or a Monday or a different day of the week—then we spend Saturday getting all our chores done. We rally around that, and everybody works to do whatever is necessary, because they know the next day is going to be a rest day.

The rest day doesn't mean the kids can't hang out with their friends or that we're together every moment of the entire day, but we are going to spend a good portion of our rest day intentionally doing things together as a family. Typically, that means that we go to church on Saturday afternoons so we don't have church on Sundays. The hustle and bustle of getting ready and serving isn't there anymore. Now, everybody wakes up on their own time, and then we go on a family date together to get coffee and pastries, and we just hang out. Sometimes we'll do an activity together, like going shopping or going out for another meal. When our house was being built, we would go over to see the progress, pray over it, and talk about what we wanted to do in the house after it was done.

Then, when we come home, we do our family calendar together. This means looking at the week to come and talking about what it looks like and what we might need to prepare. This is another step in inviting your family into your purpose, because as a family you are designing what you're doing for the upcoming week. I no longer have to text my wife, wondering what's going on, because we're all figuring out what we're doing. I might not go over every work appointment in detail, but my wife and kids know when I'm at work and I know what's going on in their lives too.

My son and daughter had been working for weeks on projects where they had to write a report about somebody in history and then give a speech about that person's life. I didn't want to miss my son dressed up as George Washington and my daughter dressed up as Elizabeth Hamilton when they did their speeches. Somehow it wasn't on my calendar, but when we went over the family calendar, I saw that it was coming up and was able to adjust my schedule so I could be there.

My family and I use a really cool resource for our calendar, called Family Teams (https://shop.familyteams.com/products/family-plan-calendar).

The Family Teams calendar is a gigantic calendar that you can hang on your refrigerator. It has all the days of the week, but it also asks questions like how you're planning to rest this week and how you're going to prepare for it. It even has a list of chores that need to get done. It's a great tool for planning your rest in addition to keeping the rest of the family schedule.

At our family meeting, we also ask:

- What are you grateful for?
- What are we going to pray for?
- What's our word of the week going to be?

Our word of the week is usually a character trait or something for all of us to focus on that week. We rarely repeat it or discuss it throughout the week, but we take the time each Sunday to create an intentional opportunity to educate our kids about different character traits, mindsets, and attitudes. For example, when I look at the schedule for the upcoming week, I might realize that we're all going to be busy and need a lot of patience, so we'll make *patience* the word of the week. I can ask the kids, "What do you think it means to be patient?" and, "How are you going to be patient this week? I might need you to help me so I can be patient, too."

I don't come to this meeting with the answers to these questions planned out; it's something we all discuss as a family. The answers change based on what we're all working on and by looking at our week ahead—but they all come back to helping us fulfill our family purpose of loving others.

QUARTERLY REST

There are two really important ways you have to rest quarterly, one with your coworkers or team, and one individually.

Individually

My mentor in college used to take what he called DAWG days—Days Alone with God—where he would just go out and be alone in the wilderness to rest.

To be honest, I tried this a couple of times—I borrowed my dad's truck, drove up to the lake, and camped overnight by myself—but this wasn't very restful for me; I get anxious in that kind of environment (and the sun comes up early, so I couldn't sleep in!). I don't really like camping so trying it was fine, but it wasn't restful.

However, I'm a big advocate of doing something alone once a quarter, regardless of what that looks like. It might be reading, doing research, or sitting in silence. It's usually just for a couple hours, not an all-day thing. I don't go to a cabin on my own or anything. I love to golf and usually make it a community activity, but when it's 110 degrees in the blazing Arizona sun, nobody else wants to be on the golf course—but I love it. I'm from Arizona, so the heat doesn't bother me, and I appreciate getting to play on beautiful golf courses with no one around.

Some of your best thinking happens when you're alone with your thoughts. Have you ever been in the shower or stuck in traffic and suddenly solved a problem you weren't even thinking about, but the solution just came to you? Taking larger blocks of intentional alone time can increase that exponentially!

When your mind isn't focused on your normal, day-to-day tasks, it has the freedom to think and go in different directions. Your creativity can be taken to higher levels and you can unlock problem-solving skills that were previously hidden. Take individual time to go at a different pace so that when you go back to your normal rhythms, you're a more effective contributor.

As a Team

One of the ways I like to rest with my team is by playing golf together. We also do a service project every quarter, which doesn't sound like rest, but it's outside of what we normally do at work. We take a break from our phones and computers and daily tasks and go to the food bank to package food boxes.

Doing something outside of what you normally do is important to relationship building. If you're not a team leader, manager, or business owner, you can do this on your own with your coworkers. Ask them if they want to play golf on a Saturday morning. Go out to eat together. Maybe try a development day together, where everyone comes into the office but you don't work on your regular tasks. Instead, take an online course together, listen to an audiobook or a podcast, or even just be in the same space reading books or doing some continuing education. This doesn't even have to be a whole day—it can be just a couple of hours—just as long as everyone is taking time away from their normal routine and getting some time to rest together.

This only happens four times a year, so if you're a business owner or manager who thinks you can't do this with your team because you need to grind them and work them every hour, understand that people perform better when they have social engagement, and you'll all perform better with rest. For more on that you can check out my previous book, *The Problem Isn't Their Paycheck: How to Attract Top Talent and Build a Thriving Company Culture.*

ANNUAL REST

Amy Porterfield likes to say, "Almost everything will start working again if you unplug it, wait for a while, then plug it back in." And she's right! This is also why I strongly recommend taking at least a week every year to completely unplug from your normal work. And unplugged means all the way unplugged—for me, that's no social media, no email, rarely do I even pick up my phone. (An "unplug" week is also mandatory for everyone in my office.)

Again, to be completely honest, this is really hard for me.

Even though I take two months "off" every year (and I try to do my unplugged week in September, while I'm on vacation with my family), I get anxious when I try to sit in awkward silence—and that's okay.

Once my mind breaks through that anxiety, it goes to places it doesn't normally go, and that helps me come up with some of my best ideas for my business. I have some of the most amazing breakthroughs during these times, so the week unplugged every year is huge for me and my personal well-being, and it's also huge for my business.

Schedule this week as part of your ideal year calendar, so you can be sure it actually happens.

Every year, I try to take different sections of my team—especially my sales staff—to a conference together. This is time for learning, fun, and for me to be able to bless them. We go out to eat at nice restaurants and enjoy some new experiences while we're away.

We create conversations around what we are learning at the conference and take the opportunity to network with other people in the same spaces as us so we can learn more about what's happening in the industry.

We rarely take the time to do these things in the day-to-day, but we make time and put ourselves in that environment.

You can also do this in your personal life. I have friends, a married couple, who love to attend marriage conferences every year. Their marriage is amazing, they love each other well, and they're constantly growing. As a result, one of their annual rhythms has become a respite from their day-to-day, just to take some time to intentionally focus on their marriage.

TAKE TIME FOR YOURSELF

There are ten different life domains:

1. Financial
2. Vocational
3. Intellectual
4. Emotional
5. Physical
6. Social
7. Marital
8. Parental
9. Spiritual
10. Avocational

Many people forget about the avocational domain. I did. I didn't have an avocational goal for so long. I worked, spent time with my family, and served, but I didn't have anything I did and tried to get better at on my own.

My business coach, Michael Hyatt, told me that I needed an

avocational goal. My first reaction was, "That's dumb. I'm doing fine without one!" But I reluctantly did it anyway. However, when it came to choosing my avocational goal, I had a hard time choosing something. I really like to work, but I had to write something down as a goal that was not work or family related. Finally, under pressure, I reluctantly wrote, "Surf?"

At the time, I was an almost-forty-year-old man living in Arizona...where there's no ocean. But as I have previously mentioned, I regularly spend time in California, and I've always kind of wanted to try surfing, so I bought an inflatable surfboard and learned to surf...kind of. I learned to stand up, but it wasn't pretty. I got torn up in the waves several times, and had to take many breaks just to catch my breath, but it was something to have fun with. I worked at surfing and tried to get better, but it was great to have something with no stakes involved. If I sucked at it and failed, nothing bad was going to happen.

That's what an avocational goal does. There's zero pressure; it's just you having a thing you do without a whole lot of pressure, just for fun—no stakes involved.

This avocational goal changed so many other things. My mind started operating differently and I started to perform better.

Your entire work is not just about work and your family. You need to have something avocational for yourself, too. Intentionally pursuing something fun or having a hobby is rest because it breaks you out of your work-and-family-mode routine and gives you an opportunity to grow.

And, hey, if you try something and it doesn't work out...it is perfectly okay to switch hobbies. I realized that I am never going to become a surfer dude, and now my hobby is golf. Fore!

ADDITIONAL THOUGHTS

Recognize that there are things in your life that may prevent you from resting.

For me, sometimes one of those things is my phone. So when I go home, I have a place where I put my phone so I can take a rest from that technology. Sometimes I need a rest from my laptop, so I put that away too.

Identify the things in your life that prevent you from resting and then create an intentional rhythm or trigger to put them on pause. I'm not saying to take away your phone or laptop forever, just take a little break so you can get some rest.

As with so many other things we've discussed, I want to emphasize that none of this happens 100 percent of the time. We're lucky if it happens 70 percent of the time—but that's way better than never doing it. No one succeeds perfectly all the time; life just doesn't work that way. Just do your best. There's no shame if you don't get to do all the rest you planned, especially resting one full day every week.

There's also no guilt in sleeping in. In fact, I think people who sleep in have a superpower, and I feel bad for people who wake up at four in the morning to grind and work, work, work. I like to work too, but I need—and also like!—to sleep.

Finally, it's okay to think about work when you're on vacation. Sometimes when I'm on my unplugged week, while my wife is reading a book next to me, my brother-in-law Dan is listening to Dave Matthews, and my kids are jumping in the waves, I sit and think about work. And that's okay. In fact, it's more than okay; it's praiseworthy. Work is worship, because God created me to contribute. And you can hold work in your mind even when you're resting. Breaking out of those regular rhythms and routines lets me look at things differently.

I don't feel stressed that I'm not enjoying vacation enough or worry that I shouldn't be thinking about work. I'm not anxious about other things I need to do; I just relax and think about ways to potentially help me do my work better when I return from that vacation, which is awesome.

REBUTTALS

"Grant, I can't rest. I'm always thinking about work, and I'm anxious if I'm told I can't think about it."

You were created to contribute. There's no shame in wanting to work, in being good at it, or in enjoying it. I mean, a whole chapter in this book is dedicated to the concept of purposeful work; you're never going to hear me tell you that you can't or shouldn't think about work.

So, that's not what I'm saying here. What I am saying is that everything works better with rest. If you like work, you will rest because when you do so intentionally, it makes your work better. It makes your work more impactful, more productive, and more fun.

"I don't have time to do all these things. I can't schedule work and time with my family and the things I want to do *and* rest."

The reality is that you have to make time for rest or you will burn out. Your body will crash, and then you will be forced to rest—and that will be reactive.

But when you are proactive about your rest—when you intentionally schedule it—you are actually able to work more because you are better able to focus, so you are more productive. When you are passive about rest, your need for that rest takes over, and that's when you find yourself scrolling TikTok for an hour or binge-watching four episodes of a show without realizing it—and then feeling guilty because you spent so much time doing nothing.

You can have time for rest, and you can be spontaneous about it, too. It doesn't all have to be scheduled, but more often than not it should be proactive and built into the rhythms of your life.

"I can't take an entire week off to unplug every year. That's just not necessary."

You don't know how necessary it is until you do it. It unleashes so many different areas of your mind that you didn't even realize you weren't tapping into. Your mind is amazing and capable of more than you give it credit for, but it's also designed to rest. So when you intentionally and fully unplug for a week, your mind works differently and comes up with even more awesome stuff.

Look, I know it's going to be weird at first. You might start and then want to stop because it's hard to be silent or you get anxious. I do too. It's awkward the first couple of days— and that's okay. By the time that week is over, I'm always so pumped that I did it because I get so much out of my mind that I otherwise wouldn't have. And that allows me to jump into the next work phase so much sharper and more focused.

I noticed that my team wasn't taking their week fully unplugged, because they were working hard and pursuing our purpose. They like to work, and they know it makes a difference. And it adds value to their life, so why would they want to stop? They might go on vacation and work less, but they were all still working. There's nothing wrong with that, but I believe that everybody needs a full week once a year to completely unplug, so I implemented it as a requirement. Now it's something we talk about; we ask each other, "So when's your week unplugged?"

Things still come up before and after you want to take time off, so be aware of that. Trust in your team while you're away (needless to say, most businesses probably don't want everyone to take their week unplugged at the same time!), and give yourself some grace. The world won't fall apart if you stop working for a week. If you have customers or people on your team who you feel absolutely need you twenty-four hours a day, seven days a week, you have the wrong customers or the wrong team members. The same is true if they can't support you taking seven days—out of 365—to unplug. I don't want people on my team who are going to get mad if I take a week away. I want people who understand that, who have grace for me during that time, and who step in and help.

Everyone needs rest, and resting will allow all of us to live out our work purpose even better.

"I feel guilty or selfish when I sleep in or take time away from work to rest. People are depending on me!"

You're right. People are dependent on you, and that's good. But you need to be your best for those people, and the only way to be at your best is by intentionally, proactively resting.

"I don't have enough time in my day! It feels like the time to rest has to come from somewhere. If you're not telling me to work less, where is this time supposed to come from? Where do I start?"

One of the reasons you probably feel like you don't have enough time is because you are in high demand. A lot of people depend on you, you're good at what you do, and you have tons of obligations at the office or your place of work.

Start with one thing you can control, something that feels doable. Rest will help you be more efficient in the other areas of your life; see Chapter 4 for more efficiency tips to give you back even more time. As you get better at planning and scheduling, you can find more time for rest.

The best place to start is by making sure you're getting good sleep. It may be hard to sleep in when you feel like you have to get up and get things done, but if you can make the most of the time you already spend in bed, that can make a big difference.

Some simple ways to get better sleep are to dramatically lower your caffeine intake throughout the day and stop drinking caffeinated beverages earlier in the day. Try eating healthier, more natural and real foods in the evening and being physically active as many days as possible. All of this will help you sleep better.

From there, try to take one day of rest from your work, like my family Sabbath day. That's another great place to start because you're spending more time with the people you love and you're all resting together, whatever that looks like for each of you.

If you feel like taking a week off is too long, start with a long weekend. Or look at where you have a three-day weekend because of a holiday and try to add a day to that. Try those four days and, eventually, go for five days. You can do this!

"How do I get my family to rest with me on family rest days?"

Make those family rest days something to look forward to. My kids look forward to getting a pastry at the coffee shop— it's amazing how something as simple as a little sugar can help get them on board! Are my kids always pumped up every time we do the family calendar? No, sometimes it's like, "Oh, we have to do this." And that's okay! Sometimes we just have to do our routines grudgingly. You might go kicking and screaming into your week unplugged—and that's okay, too. As long as you do it.

"I don't have an avocation or a hobby, and if I don't have one by now I think I'm too old to pick up something new."

I was thirty-eight when I picked up my hobby, and it wasn't easy. I fell off my surfboard a *ton*. And it took a global pandemic to get me to pick up golfing! I'm not going to tell you that it's going to be easy, just that *it's okay* if it's hard or if it doesn't come naturally to you. It's still super valuable to try something new.

And if you try something and don't like it, try something else. Maybe you don't like golf or surfing, but you want to try playing an instrument, baking, or writing short stories. Great! Try it, and give yourself some grace. It's okay not to be good at it, and it's okay not to do it forever. Remember, the point of an avocational life domain is to engage in an activity without any stakes involved.

A LITTLE BIT SOFTER NOW

Think about that song "Shout." You've probably heard it at just about every wedding you've ever attended.

When that song comes on everyone is ready to have a good

time and starts to dance their butts off. Even the awkward uncle who doesn't normally dance is out on the dance floor sweating through his shirt. But then it gets "a little bit softer now, a little bit softer now, a little bit softer now," and everyone slows down. They all rest. This is the time to take a breath, with your tongue hanging out, laughing with other people. The song isn't over, but everything is softer.

And then momentum builds back up. Soon enough, here we go again, everything is getting a little louder and then a little louder still. Ties are coming off, sweat's dripping, everybody is smiling and shouting along, jumping and having a great time—maybe even a better time than towards the beginning of the song, because the best part comes after some rest. With that momentum, you can go bigger, be greater, and have even more impact.

KEY TAKEAWAYS

- Make a plan to get enough rest—and especially plenty of sleep—every day, week, quarter, and year. Consider trying a new hobby as a way to take an intentional break from your daily routine.
- Consider which of your weekly rhythms also serve as rest for you and your family, and make sure to prepare ahead of time to ensure that rest can happen consistently!
- Try to take a day (or part of a day) each quarter to rest on your own and another day to rest with your team, doing something outside of your typical tasks. Once a year, take a week completely unplugged from your regular work.

MY INTENTIONAL ACTIONS

A QUICK WIN: GIVE 'EM A REST

One of the biggest successes in my marriage came after I recognized that my wife also needed to start taking a day of rest on her own.

Day in and day out, she was grinding and working, wiping heinies, cleaning up Cheerios, breaking up fights, and being Super Mom. But she needs time to just be a human being for a while. And when I didn't give her that time, it was rough.

So I took time out of my schedule to take over her duties for at least half a day every week. At first, she would drop off the babies at the office, and I would try to work and be a dad at the same time. I usually didn't get a lot of work done, but she had four or five hours to herself, where she could just *be*. Sometimes, now that they're older, I take the kids for a whole day on the weekend.

I did my best to tell her not to run errands during that time. She felt like that was the only time she had to get things done without the kids, but running errands wasn't rest for her. Eventually, I impressed upon her that she needs that rest too. Don't do stuff you normally have to do.

She felt valued that I was making sure she had rest, and that was a game changer for our marriage and our family.

Rest is hard to execute if everyone is not supporting it. Look for places where you can give your spouse or partner some time to rest in the way that is most meaningful for them, whether that's taking a nap, scrolling social media, going shopping, or doing something avocational. Recognize the rhythms of rest *they* need to be at their best, and do what you can to support them implementing those rhythms. When you create a rhythm that intentionally gives your spouse rest, they will respond in kind by supporting a rhythm for your rest.

CHAPTER 6

EVALUATION

What kind of lead singer do you want to be? The one who comes off stage and yells at everybody about the mistakes they made during the performance, or the one who leads everyone back onstage for an encore because the crowd is going wild?

Do you want to have a one-hit wonder, or do you want to generate hit after hit so people flock by the thousands to come watch you play? Be like Elvis, the Beatles, even Ozzy Osbourne or the Rolling Stones (who can barely stand up anymore, but their shows keep getting better and better).

YOU ARE ON A JOURNEY

Pursuing purpose is a journey, not a destination. You can never arrive at having perfect work–life harmony. But you can always make the song better. This isn't a class where you get to the end of the semester and then graduate. This is life—*your* life—and you can always improve.

In fact, any time you think you're doing something perfectly is dangerous. In order to make the biggest impact possible, we need to be constantly improving. We are imperfect and constantly changing, so we need to adjust with those changes and strive to get better. Even if you feel like you did something 100 percent perfectly, you will at the very least need to make adjustments for the changes happening in society and within you in the future.

Understanding that you can learn how to get better, and doing so, is the key to growth. If someone says, "I did it all right," they have zero room for growth. As a result, they'll stay stagnant while everyone else around them who thinks they could do better has the chance to grow.

And I'm not just talking about business; I'm also talking about your family. No one likes to grow alone. When growth happens together, it's more sustainable. In a marriage, it's difficult if one spouse is growing and the other is not. It can create competition and jealousy. Or can anyone out there honestly say, "I'm the best parent there is and there are zero ways I can improve my parenting"? No, of course not. We can always get better—and you should *want* to get better because when you are a better parent, you give your children a better chance to have a big impact on society, to choose the right career or spouse, to make really wise choices and become their own amazing human beings.

You have to grow as a leader in order to help those around you grow, too. You don't want to limit your impact. I'm sure I'd never hear you say, "I only want to help people *this much*," or, "I only want to have a little bit of impact on my community." No, you believe that your work matters and your purpose is important and that you can make a great impact on people...so why not make the *greatest possible* impact on those people?

If you want to grow to the next level and make the biggest impact possible, here's the hard truth: you need to evaluate your progress. I say that not to discourage you, but so you realize that you don't have to do all of this at once. Don't look at this book and think, "Oh my gosh, I have so much work to do. How am I going to be able to take on all of this?"

I started and then I got better and better because I kept evaluating how I was doing. I figured out the next step in my journey, and then I took it.

Start small, but start somewhere. Then evaluate how you did, and continue to get better, to make progress and improve. Add on a little bit more, bit by bit, year after year, until eventually you get to a place where you look back and realize, "Holy cow, I'm *really* good at this!"

Don't compare your progress to mine. I've been intentionally trying to have work–life harmony for more than fifteen years, as of the writing of this book. My journey is going to look different than yours—and that's a good thing. You can learn from my mistakes and do some of the things I struggled with more easily. If this is your first year, or even your first day, of intentionally pursuing work–life harmony, that's great! You get a head start because now you can learn from the mistakes I've made and the successes I've had—and it probably won't take you fifteen years to get there. It'll take time, but I hope to save you some time too.

I think all of us have decided to try something new. Maybe you said, "I'm going to try to play the guitar." Maybe you even went as far as graduating from playing *Guitar Hero* on the Xbox to going into Guitar Center and buying a guitar. Then you start to play and your fingers hurt. You suck at it, and it's hard. Finally, you just say, "Screw it," and shove the guitar in a corner of your garage, where it sits collecting dust.

You have to have grace for yourself, for even giving it a shot and trying something new. You're not going to be perfect. You're going to make mistakes. And it might even hurt a little. But having that built-in grace for yourself and evaluating your progress to figure out what you can focus on next to keep getting better makes it less overwhelming—and it helps you ensure you don't quit, especially in the areas that are most important to you. Maybe you're never going to be the next Jon Bon Jovi...but you can still be a rock star to your family and at work.

FOUR QUESTIONS TO EVALUATE EVERYTHING

I don't believe that evaluating your progress needs to be complicated. I'm not going to make this a grand inquisition or give you a seventy-two-point inspection sheet. It's not going to take months to answer. Instead, we're going to keep it simple and straightforward so that it's actually doable. (In fact, you'll be able to memorize this evaluation process by the end of this chapter so you're ready to implement it in every area of your life.)

I believe that you evaluate each area of your life with these four questions:

- What do I need to add?
- What do I need to remove?
- What do I need to do more of?
- What do I need to do less of?

But wait! Before we look at these four questions in more detail, I need a commitment from you. I need you to promise that you will not go through this evaluation process and add more than one answer per question. You're going to be tempted to come up with multiple answers for each question, but then your list of things to change becomes way too long—and that becomes discouraging and hard to remember, and makes it impossible for you to focus on actually *making* the changes. If you give yourself too much to do, your effort and energy are spread too thin.

But when you only make a reasonable number of changes, you can have the focus to make the impact and progress you want to make. And here's the good news: if you do come up with more than one answer you really like, just pick one now and you can use the other one next time!

And this evaluation process is not about adding more to your plate. You add one thing, but you remove something else, so it's a net even. You do more of one thing, but less of another, so you are not using additional time, energy, and effort—you are maximizing what you already do so you can have the greatest impact.

Do I have your promise? Great! Let's look at each of the questions in more detail.

WHAT DO I NEED TO ADD?

When most people hear this question, they think of the negative first. "Oh no, there are so many things I'm not doing."

Your answer to this question should be something you know you need to be doing, but you're not. Maybe you tried it once and quit. Maybe you see other people doing it and know you should be too. Maybe it's even something you read in this book! In fact, you probably already knew what your answer should be as soon as you read the question. It's the obvious one, the one that your gut or heart or brain is telling you to do.

Some examples here could include praying with your spouse, adding weekly dates with your kids, intentionally apologizing for something as a parent once a week, adding a purpose to your work, or creating your ideal year calendar. The thing you choose to add is completely up to you, and it'll be different for everyone. I can't tell you which one to pick; it has to be that one thing that stands out most for you.

You're going to evaluate again and again, which we'll talk about later in the chapter, so you're not stuck if you pick the "wrong" answer here. Just pick one and if you want to change it next time, that's fine. But hopefully you pick one and it becomes a habit, and then you add something else the next time around.

WHAT DO I NEED TO REMOVE?

There's also something in your life that you need or want to remove. This is important because when most people evaluate their goals, they tend to focus only on adding things to their lives and fail to remove anything. That's just going to lead to overwhelm; you also have to find something to remove.

As with the first question, your answer to this question will likely be fairly obvious. It's something you're currently doing that you shouldn't be doing or don't need to be doing. It's a time-waster or something that causes guilt or shame in your life. It needs to be removed from your life because it's impacting your relationship with your spouse, children, or business.

Some examples here might include removing phones at the dinner table, removing anger from your reactions when your kids do something specific that grates on you, or removing the focus on money at work.

I like to use a system or trigger to help me remember this or to keep me accountable. When I wanted to use my phone less, I designated a specific place to put my phone as soon as I walked in the door each day. If you want to stay off your phone while you're in bed, try setting up your router to turn off the Wi-Fi every night before your bedtime. If you are trying to remove debt, you may want to create a paper chain with every link representing a certain amount of money, so you can rip off a link every time you pay off that amount. Watching that chain, and your debt, shrink will make you excited to keep going.

Just saying "I'm going to remove this" is not going to make it happen. But by getting some help removing it, and using triggers or other hacks, you are more likely to be successful.

The thing you remove doesn't have to feel like you're doing something crappy and you need to get rid of it. Maybe you have a lot of great things going on but you need more margin in your life, so you remove something even though it's a good thing. My wife and I intentionally stopped doing small group at church. We get connection and grow at church, but we already have so many relationships and are in community with so many people that the smaller in-home group was just one more thing to commit to every week. We were spread too thin. It's okay to remove something good in order to create more space for all the other good things you have going on.

WHAT DO I NEED TO DO MORE OF?

There's always something in each area of my life that I want to do more of because it's good, it's working well, and I want to keep doing it. You may have started doing this thing intentionally or not, but you want to continue doing it—and to do more of it—intentionally now. Give yourself credit for the good thing you've been doing.

I want to be clear that this is not the same as adding something new; this is something you are already doing that you want to do more of.

Maybe you want to celebrate your clients more, so you use social media to see when they have something major happen in their lives so you can send them a card or a gift. Maybe you want to build more connection with your family, so on your day of rest together you decide to also have a fun breakfast every week. Maybe you already go on an anniversary trip but you want to give more meaning and depth to it, so you do these evaluation questions with your spouse.

WHAT DO I NEED TO DO LESS OF?

Finally, there's also something that you probably need to do less of. You don't necessarily have to remove it, but you probably shouldn't do it as much.

Let me set one expectation right away: this is always the hardest question to answer. Often, when you think of something to do less of, there's a tendency to think that you might as well just remove it entirely. But you've already chosen something to remove, and the goal of doing this evaluation is not to either add or remove a ton of stuff, because that would be really hard and require a ton of work. Alternately, people think that if they are doing less of something, they have to replace it with something else. Don't fall into that trap! That only adds more stress and work here—you're already doing more of something, and that's why you want to do less of something else.

So think of something that isn't necessarily bad, and there's certainly no shame in doing it, but it's something you just don't need or want to do as much.

For example, if you binge-watch a lot of Netflix after the kids go to sleep, or if as a family you're watching too much TV, you may choose to watch less. There's nothing wrong with watching TV, but what would it look like to do less of it?

Or maybe you always eat lunch alone at your desk and you still want to do that some of the time, just less often. Once or twice a week, you're going to take your lunch into the break room and eat when other people are having lunch, so you can take part in that community.

Maybe your family eats out or gets a lot of takeout. There's nothing wrong with that, but you may decide that instead of eating out four times a week, you want to save money and eat a little better, so you only eat out twice a week.

Similarly, there's nothing wrong with working at home, but

you may choose to put boundaries around it and do less of it. Maybe you want to drink less coffee so you can get better sleep.

EXAMPLES OF EVALUATION IN ACTION

Again, you are choosing only one answer for each of these four questions. Those answers should be simple enough that you can remember them but, nonetheless, write all of your answers on one Post-it note and stick it somewhere you can see it every day.

I answer these questions in each of my priority areas in my life, so I actually have four answers in four areas, which means sixteen answers overall. Let me show you some examples of evaluations I have done in each of these life priorities.

MARRIAGE

When my wife and I get away for our annual anniversary trip, we break away from our normal everyday life and celebrate that we made it another year. Then we go through these four questions together.

Recently, our answers included more family dinners throughout the week, less cell phone time while in the house, adding a Botma BBQ every other month when our friends and their kids can come over and have community, and removing serving from one area of church because we were serving in that area too much and were stretched too thin.

PARENTING

Now that my kids are older, I ask them some version of these four questions when I take them on their birthday trips.

- How am I doing as a dad?
- What can I do to be a better dad?
- What's something I do right now as a dad that you love, that I should keep doing?
- What's something that I'm not doing very well? Or, what's something that you wish I changed?

When I ask some version of what I need to do more of or how I'm doing as a dad, for example, my kids tell me that they love our weekly dates. It's not like, "You need to take us on more trips to Disneyland." They just like spending time together.

The important thing is to ask the questions and then just listen and take notes. It's not about arguing with your children or getting defensive or frustrated and trying to change their minds. Above all, when this conversation is over, you want your kids to know that you love them—and also that they can talk to you. One of the best ways for kids to learn that is to show them. Ask questions and listen, without cutting them off or offering rebuttals. Look them in the eyes and pay attention to them. Focusing on them is one of the ways they know how much you love them. (And you're demonstrating humility and evaluation for them, so they see that you are always trying to do better.)

When my daughter Cambria and I first started talking about these questions, it was hard for her. She didn't really know what they meant. But in the past couple of years, she's started to appreciate the conversation more. I've taken the time to build up trust and equity so she feels comfortable talking to me. And, because she knows the questions are coming, she is more prepared for them each year.

Recently, she told me, "Daddy, I don't like it when you raise your voice," and she gave me an example of when I raised my voice after she hadn't obeyed me right away. I do that naturally; I have a loud voice. And I consider obedience a matter of respect, and I don't like feeling that I or my wife are being disrespected. But when Cambria said that, it made me realize that I can probably parent first-time obedience without raising my voice, and maybe even do it in a more impactful way. Instead of yelling, I now try to take her aside, one on one, look her in the eye, and talk to her very seriously. And boom! It changed everything. Her first-time obedience dramatically increased, our relationship got better, and she was hurt and frustrated a lot less because she had previously shut down when I unknowingly raised my voice.

WORK

At our annual retreats, the Stewardship co-founders and I ask the same four questions, but we add a fifth:

- What's your vision for the next ten years?

We don't set ten-year goals because life changes so fast that they will likely look different in five years. But we work really hard at creating the goals for the next twelve months and asking these questions.

One year, we said we wanted to have more connections and community involvement. We wanted fewer Swiss-Army-knife employees (meaning employees who did many different things in a lot of different areas), so we worked to find out what they enjoy and where they work well, so we could have them focus more on that. We wanted to add certain specific pieces of content: one year it was live events, and another year we removed a specific referral source because we didn't like the types of referrals that were being sent our way and the attitude that referral source gave us in the process.

REST/SELF-REFLECTION

Most of the things I add, remove, do more of, or do less of have to do with rhythms or efficiency. I recognize that something isn't working well in one of those rhythms and look at the specifics when deciding how to answer those questions for myself. If you are having a hard time determining where to start with evaluation, look at your rhythms.

NOT ONE AND DONE

Before I have these discussions or spend time in self-reflection I spend time preparing beforehand so I can come ready with my answers to the questions. When I know I have these evaluation questions coming up, I take notes in an app on my phone. Most importantly, I prepare to put everything else on pause so I can focus on the person or people I am with (or myself!). It takes intentional time and work to do that.

When I have these evaluations with adults, such as my wife and co-founders, they know that these questions are coming up. I ask them to please be prepared for these conversations as well. My kids aren't adults, but they're picking up on the fact that this is a time where we talk about how Daddy's doing.

At this evaluation stage, what I'm really asking is, "How are we doing in meeting our purpose?" What do we need to do more of, do less of, add, and remove as it pertains to loving them better (not just generally)? All those purposes—work, family, and life—are connected, and the purpose gives direction to these meetings.

When you do this, it's more than just asking yourself the questions and then writing out the answers. You also want to think through the next step you have to take in order to make those changes come to life.

For example, when my wife and I decided to use our cell phones less at home, we took the next step together before our anniversary trip ended. We decided to get a box where we could put our phones away whenever we enter the house—and then we ordered the box online so it would be delivered around the same time we returned home.

Ask yourself, "What's my next action?" and then take it.

Most importantly, if you want to have better work–life harmony, don't just evaluate one time; continue evaluating on a regular basis. I recommend making a rhythm of doing this evaluation process once a year. You don't want to evaluate too often because that doesn't give you enough time to actually make the change you're evaluating.

Set aside some time annually to review your ideal year calendar, your rhythms and efficiencies, and your purpose. Do this with your spouse, your children, and your work, and also with yourself, in your own life.

CELEBRATE THE WINS

I want to emphasize that evaluation is not just about thinking, "Where did I go wrong?" Evaluation is about trying to repeat what you did well, so you can keep doing more of that.

Evaluation gives you an opportunity to celebrate when you are doing things that align with your purpose. If you're not celebrating your wins, you're not going to want to continue pursuing those purposes. But when you do celebrate, you *are* a winner. Celebration during evaluation makes evaluation a lot more fun!

And celebrating is how you make memories. Go out for ice cream or get pizza. Go on vacation. Do whatever feels like an indulgence for you. Tell your family, "We just did a great job of meeting and living by our purpose in [such and such area]. Let's celebrate that!"

These are the types of memories you want to fill your life with—and the lives of those around you. Your spouse, your kids, your coworkers—celebrate your wins with all of them.

REBUTTALS

"How am I going to make this all happen? How am I supposed to find time for this?"

Intentionally schedule it. When you do your ideal year calendar, you're going to schedule evaluation automatically as part of that process. Create your ideal year calendar, or at least a rough draft of it, so you can go to your spouse, children, and business partners/team and invite everybody into it.

Once you begin, this process will start to snowball. It gets easier to make changes. And because you're waiting to implement these changes only once per year, you can get excited for it and look forward to them.

"It seems like too much pressure and buildup to do this on anniversary trips. I just want to enjoy my time with my spouse."

It doesn't have to happen on the trip. It can happen over dinner or on a walk. Talk while you're driving or on the plane. Sometimes we ask these questions while we're just hanging out in bed. There's no official way of doing this, mandated time to do so, or perfect moment. Sometimes we're having so much fun on an anniversary trip we just speed through the answers. Doing it is better than not doing it at all, and there's no perfect way.

"I have all these things I need to add. Where do I start?"

Focus on just adding one per major life area or priority. If you're trying to add more than one, there's a very good chance you won't get to it.

"Do I need to make a spreadsheet or a Gantt chart?"

Nope, this doesn't need to be a big process. Take some notes, on paper or in an app. If the process is complicated, you're doing it wrong. You should be able to write all of your answers on one Post-it note, even if that means boiling your answers down to just a word or two.

"Isn't this *too* easy? Will just asking four questions actually make a change?"

Not only will this have an impact, it will have a *bigger* impact by limiting it to one answer for each of these four questions because that allows you to focus and make the change happen with more intention. You only have so much time and energy, so use it to its greatest effect.

YOUR SONG

Your evaluation isn't going to look like mine because your relationship with your spouse, kids, and coworkers doesn't look like mine. Your business isn't like mine. And that's the beautiful thing about life, and about music. Everyone doesn't sing the same song in the same way, but they can still have harmony. I want you to have your own song, with its own harmony, and you can only discover what's best for you by trying it out.

You are going to hear from my wife in the next chapter about what she thinks of all of this. She doesn't pull any punches, so you'll hear when it's been annoying and what she's found valuable on our family's journey to work–life harmony.

KEY TAKEAWAYS

- Answer four questions for evaluation in each area of your life:
  - What do I need to add?
  - What do I need to remove?
  - What do I need to do more of?
  - What do I need to do less of?
- Perform this evaluation at least once per year with your spouse, your children, your work, and also on your own. Prior to or during these evaluations, review your ideal year calendar, your rhythms and efficiencies, and your purpose.
- Celebrate your progress and the wins you make each year, with your family, at work, and with anyone whose support contributes to your ongoing success.

MY INTENTIONAL ACTIONS

A QUICK WIN: ASK THEM TO EVALUATE YOU

It's one thing to evaluate yourself and to evaluate with others; it's another thing entirely to invite people to evaluate *you*.

Ask your spouse, partner, and/or kids to evaluate you: "How am I doing as a spouse? How am I doing as a parent?"

Follow that question up with, "What's something I'm doing that I should keep doing? What's something I should be doing differently?"

This may be difficult because you have to ask the question and be open to the answer. Depending on how you've responded to criticism or critical thinking conversations in the past, your kids or your spouse may not trust you not to get angry or defensive. If that's your reality, it doesn't mean you shouldn't execute this quick win; it means you should repeat it *more often* because the more often you're asking these questions and the more recent instances of positive engagement they have with you when they do answer, the more your relationship will heal and the more likely they will be to respond to the questions in the future.

Some of the best, hardest-hitting pieces of evaluation I've ever received about myself have come from asking other people, "How am I doing?" If I'm honest, I didn't agree with all of the feedback, and it was hard to hear—but, dang it, there has been a lot that was right on.

Be prepared for that. It's fun for people to tell us encouraging, loving, supportive words to lift us up, but that's not always what evaluation is. This isn't mean; it's critical feedback, and that isn't bad. You have to receive critical feedback to be able to evaluate. We all have flaws and ways that we can improve. The willingness and action to humbly seek critical feedback is good!

Likely the safest relationship in your life—and the one that may need evaluation more than anywhere else—is with your spouse or partner. So start there. Ask them, "How can I get better?"

CHAPTER 7

THE SUPPORTIVE SPOUSE

Many people ask me how their spouse is going to react when they are invited into a new purpose. You may have even been reading up to this point wondering, "How much of this is real?"

Well, I've asked my wife, Jodie, to share her thoughts, in her own words, about work-life harmony, about my failures and successes, and about each of the chapters you've read. I didn't tell her what to write; this is all authentic, and it's all her, so you can see how work-life harmony plays out from a spouse's perspective.

This chapter is intentionally shorter than the previous ones you've read. My wife makes fun of how long my social media posts are—she always tells me to be more concise—so her chapter is going to get right to the point.

Take it away, Jodie!

OUR FAMILY'S JOURNEY TO WORK-LIFE HARMONY

From the time Grant first started talking about opening his own finance company, and eventually growing it to what it is now, I never doubted him or worried about the finances—even though he was leaving his stable job and I was making very little money as a teacher at a Christian school. It was never an issue for me, and I think a big reason for that was because of his purpose in starting the company. It was so far beyond doing this so we could be rich or because he wanted to be the big, powerful owner of a company. He was passionate about wanting to undo the way things had been done in the industry. Grant wants to help people and set them up for success. He wants to love people through finances, genuinely. That's a no-brainer; of course I knew he was going to be able to meet his purpose.

Because I was so on board with the foundation of why he wanted to start his own company, I wasn't worried about having to make some sacrifices along the way. Sure, I knew that making sacrifices is never easy—and they weren't—but I always had peace about the business because I was so connected to the purpose.

But what *was* hard for us was when there was no plan for the schedule. When there was no end in sight of him just being at the office, working all the time, and doing everything he had to do—sometimes even spending nights on the couch in his office. At the time, I had two little children at home, and I needed him to help me parent and to give me a break. I could bring the kids to the office for an hour or two, but that usually meant he'd come home an hour or two later. That was a rough patch for me, knowing that we'd be making no money *and* my husband would be working long hours for who knows how long.

We didn't have *harmony*.

The purpose was always there, but the issue was time. I didn't feel like he made us a priority. To be honest, I thought that was part of the program. I thought it was my job to suck it up and endure it. As a result, I never communicated any of my unmet needs to him. I mean, I knew it was going to be busy. I knew the first couple of years were going to be nonstop and we wouldn't go on vacation or anything like that. I knew all of that going in—but even with those expectations, we didn't plan ways to still have work–life harmony. Honestly, I didn't even know that was *possible* in a season like this. We didn't schedule weekly date nights. We didn't make my need to have time away from the kids a priority. The weekly rhythms we now have didn't happen for so long. After all, harmony doesn't just happen by itself.

When you're starting a new business, it's hard to schedule time off; that's just the reality of it. But you can prioritize your family. You can put in effort to manage expectations. Like letting them know that this time is going to be busy and you don't see an end in sight right now, but on a specific day we will get time together, so we can all look forward to that. Or this is how I'm going to give you what you need, whether that's cleaning the house or time away from the kids. Make those part of your schedule to let your family know, *I still see you, I see your needs. I'm overwhelmed at work but I'm going to make sacrifices as well to make sure that our work-life harmony is still happening.*

Grant would come home after a long day and I would immediately hand him the kids for a while, but I didn't feel like I could take a break because I still had responsibilities. I had to make dinner and put the kids to bed. I wish I had just told Grant what I needed, because I would often get grumpy and resentful that I was with the kids all day and I still had to do the bedtime routine too. I knew Grant needed to decompress, but couldn't he do that after the kids went to bed?!

Again, I thought this was all part of the sacrifices I needed to make, that I had to carry the burdens at home while Grant carried the burdens at work. Even though I was frustrated, for the most part I just sucked it up and dealt with it.

It took some time for me to learn to tell Grant that I needed to recharge. Unless I communicated that to him, he had no idea that I needed a break from the little humans and the daily responsibilities at home. (That's what naptime is for, right??) He also had no idea about some of the internal frustrations I was dealing with either.

You need to be clear about what your needs are. Your spouse may not know unless you communicate. But don't be scared or worried or talk yourself out of it because you think it'll stress them out or they don't have time for it. You aren't going to be in harmony if one of you has needs that aren't being met.

Grant and I talked and made it clear that we needed to work together to make it happen. When you're creating your ideal year calendar and rhythms, you're not doing it in a bubble. Those rhythms affect other people, especially your family. So if one of your rhythms is that you need a day or half day off every week, that becomes part of your spouse's rhythms too. That's where harmony comes in.

With work–life harmony, our whole family is now more in the know about what's going to happen with Grant's work or our family life. We're on the same page, communication-wise and with having intentional time together, whether individually or as a family. Our life and our schedules are more predictable. There's more connection because we are intentional. The goal of harmony is to be connected and have that time together.

We go through the busy seasons with a lot more ease than we did before because we all have a better idea of what to expect. We know there's an end to those busy times, and it is easier to get through them because we know that Grant is loving and serving people, and we know that we are a part of that mission. So, in order for us to make that purpose come to life well, we all make sacrifices together.

Sometimes I tell Grant that I feel like we need to talk to the kids even more about the practical stories of what loving and serving people at Stewardship looks like. We're on board with this purpose, and the kids know this purpose, but I want them to understand what that looks like. What does loving people through finances look like practically? I like to ask him, "How did you bless somebody today?"

The other day, Grant's assistant wrote him a beautiful thank-you note, and when Grant showed it to me, I said, "We need to read this to the kids." She listed so many things about what a blessing he's been and why.

We are always working together to help the kids better understand the purpose of loving others and how it unfolds through Grant's work. Because that's exciting! And we all want to celebrate that.

JODIE ON PURPOSE

When Grant talks about his purpose, I feel like it is very much tied to our purpose as a family.

And I have always felt on board with Grant's work purpose. The whole reason he started his company in the first place was to do things differently, so he could help people with their finances with justice, integrity, and love. No matter how much we had to sacrifice in the first few years of him doing his own thing or how tough it was living on very little, I always told him, "This is beautiful. You absolutely have to keep doing this."

JODIE ON INVITING YOUR WORK AND YOUR FAMILY INTO YOUR PURPOSE

Having your family and work on board with your purpose is the first step to having work–life harmony. But I think that's impossible if you don't have a purpose that excites you and gives value to what you're doing.

If your family has no idea what you're doing at work, they just see it as you leaving and prioritizing work over them. But when your family knows about how you are meeting your purpose through that work, they can get on board and support you. I celebrate Grant and encourage him. I try to be positive about his job.

Additionally, inviting your family into your purpose keeps you grounded and helps you live for something more than yourself. If we didn't have a purpose as a family, I might want to just go live in luxury, vacation all the time, and make it all about myself! But the Lord has called us to a life that is much more meaningful than that. And our family purpose is an extension of what He has asked of us.

It's important to have a purpose when raising kids because it provides structure and a framework to so many of our daily decisions and the way we parent. Grant and I often refer to our purpose when talking with our kids, to explain why we're doing something like serving at church. It brings meaning and a common understanding to all the members of our family. It unites us. And if we ever start to stray too much from that purpose, we use it to remind each other, which allows us all to reevaluate and weed out some of the selfishness.

JODIE ON IDEAL YEARS, RHYTHMS, AND EFFICIENCIES

As a stay-at-home mom, I don't have as much structure in my day as Grant has in his. He has a lot of systems and routines in place, but I have a few rhythms and efficiencies that work for me too.

For example, I used to love to come up with different meals

and do big grocery shopping trips and buy all these ingredients, but now that just makes me feel overwhelmed, so we often eat the same style of food the majority of the time as a family. That makes it simpler for me. I was trying to make everything from scratch so it could be as healthy as possible, but I had to let go of some of that. We have three kids and I'm home with them all day, so I wanted to seriously simplify the food and cooking responsibilities. The kids also have daily and weekly chores systems, which allow them to contribute to being a part of the household—but these systems also simplify my life in many ways. It's okay to put those babies to work!

Doing our family calendar helps us to know that we have this rhythm that we repeat weekly. Family game night, intentional family time, date night for me and Grant, my time off—if we don't do our calendar on Sunday, a lot of those things we desire to have in our life don't always happen.

And it's not just writing it down; it's talking about it each week. For a while, we just put recurring appointments in our phones that said "Date Night" every Thursday. But if we didn't make a plan for those date nights to actually happen, the phone would still say Date Night, but we never got a sitter for the kids or planned what time or where we wanted to go. So having the Sunday family meetings and writing out what we all want to do each week helps us to be efficient in implementing the things we really want to happen.

The kids are really good at keeping us accountable. One of our weekly rhythms is something we call One Kid Up, where the other kids go to bed a little earlier and one kid gets to stay up later with us. We typically try to do this on Wednesday nights and put it on our calendar, but if we forget and try to schedule something else, the kids will say, "Hey, Wednesday is One Kid Up!" So engaging the whole family in the family calendar and weekly rhythms is so important to bring it all together for work–life harmony.

JODIE ON REST

Rest is absolutely underrated and under-implemented. We're so driven to get things done, people either don't see the need for rest or they think they don't have time for it. They think rest is something that can be sacrificed to be more productive, but that lack of rest will show up in your relationships and in the rest of your life.

My rest looks different from Grant's rest; we both recharge differently. It's been a journey to learn that about each other through many conversations over the fifteen years we've been married. I remember Grant once said, "When we travel, let's schedule our return trip on a Saturday so I can have Sunday off when we get back." He also asked that we not book our weekends with so many social activities because, when we overschedule, we don't have time to rest. That's something I learned to modify; I control our home-life schedule and things we're involved in or attend, and I've had to modify that over the years to respect him getting his rest so he can be at his best capacity for his work and for us.

We love Sundays to be about family. We grab some coffee, maybe go out to lunch, and then Grant likes to recharge by sitting on the couch and watching sports. This rest is what allows him to be so extremely productive and efficient during the week.

I, on the other hand, do not like sitting on the couch. That's not a restful day for me; that's a boring day. Rest for me is a break from my normal, around-the-house routines, or a day when I don't have to think about those responsibilities. Rest can also be having some alone time (I'm pretty good at ignoring Grant and the kids for a while), but I also recharge by the five of us being together. We'll often go out to eat on Sundays, or he and the kids will feed themselves, so I don't have to worry about being in the kitchen at all.

As you have probably picked up by now, Grant is the steady one in the family. His way of resting is pretty simple (and, honestly, to me it looks exactly the same all the time! Boring...), whereas what I want changes depending on how I feel, so my rest and recharge look a little different each week. No matter what it looks like, I tell Grant my desires and expectations for our rest day. And Grant respects that and tries to prioritize it.

JODIE ON EVALUATION

We go over the four questions every year around our anniversary trip in June. Starting in the spring, I start to really think about our life, our choices for our kids, and plans for the future. I think the questions we talk about are very helpful because there are always things we can change or do better.

A couple years ago, I was getting annoyed because either Grant or I would be on our phones a lot in the evenings while we were having chill time with the family. I don't know if I ever brought it up to Grant, but it was starting to bother me when I would see one of the kids come up to him and it would take him a few minutes to respond because he was engaged with whatever he was doing on his phone. So when we did our evaluation that year, and we talked about what to do less of, the answer was easy: let's spend less time on our phones. We had both realized it but hadn't had an intentional conversation about it.

When things start to frustrate one of us or we see things that need to change, whether personally, as family, or in Grant's work schedule, it all gets brought up and we talk about it. Now, knowing that we are going to discuss those questions every year, I start to anticipate them. And it looks different every single year. It's a tool to help us optimize and get better every year without being overwhelmed.

We have a safe place to talk about anything. We try to communicate all throughout the year, but sometimes you don't bring things up, whether from pride or selfishness or lack of time. You think, "I'm too tired tonight, I don't even want to start this discussion right now." So knowing that we're going to start talking about those things, we know we have to go in with humility, with prayer, ready to listen and be gracious. We try not to be nitpicky with each other and let go of the smaller stuff, but this is where we can talk about the big picture.

We homeschool our kids, so we evaluate on a family level. We're in charge of their education, so we talk about what school is going to look like, what classes they are going to do. I love that we get to know our kids and see what they need and be able to have the time to evaluate what to focus on for each of them.

Every year you want to do better. You don't always have time to just add new things into your life, so it's good to look at what to get rid of because it's not the season for us or it's taking too much or not working. This has been super powerful for our relationship and our family.

It's interesting because some years it's a thirty-minute conversation because there's not a whole lot we need to go over. Other times, it's a huge weekend with lots of conversations.

Sometimes we're talking about how many good things we have going on and we want to keep doing that.

Okay, I have already said too much. This is way longer than the bullet-point list of communication I prefer! So, I will wrap it up now and let you get back to my long-winded husband. But before I go, I would like to leave you with this one thought: work–life harmony is a process. It doesn't happen overnight. Keep working together. Keep communicating. You can do this!

SUPPORTIVE SPOUSE TIPS AND TRICKS

To ensure my wife's preferred communication style is fully lived out in this chapter, I thought it would be appropriate to provide a succinct, bullet-point list of specific tactical things we do for each other.

How Jodie supports me:

- She intentionally tries to make sure I can have a day of rest on the weekends. She doesn't ask me to do too much, and sometimes she'll say no to invites so we can just have a relaxing day off as a family.

- She knows that I like to sleep in, and she supports my circadian rhythm of getting stuff done at night and sleeping later in the morning.
- Jodie acknowledges and encourages what I do. When I do something good, she acknowledges me in a way that is genuine. At least once a week, she encourages me and tells me how great I am, which is wonderful.
- Even more importantly, she praises me in front of the kids. She'll talk about how awesome I am or what a great job I'm doing in front of the kids, at dinner or when we're all in the car. That makes a big difference, because it's not coming from me. I don't have to say, "Hey, guys, I did this awesome thing!" When she says it about me, it carries a bigger impact.
- She knows my burdens and works to give me a break.

And here are some ways I support her:

- I make sure we get a date night once a week.
- Jodie's love languages are quality time, service, and gifts. It's important to her that I know how she feels loved, and I can focus on those.
- I also make sure to give her time each week, at least half a day (if not an entire day!) where she can just do the things she *wants* to do.
- I try to take on some of her responsibilities without her having to ask me to do them for her, just to give her more of a break too.

- I adapt my work schedule to allow time for our family and the activities we want to do.
- I encourage her to pursue her individual interests. Just the other day, I got her two stand-up paddleboards so she can go for a lake day with her friends—and I worked from home that day, so I could be there with the kids.
- We do Family Fridays once a month, where we just hang out together as a family and do something fun. The first time we ever did this, we went to a Cubs game. But most Family Fridays are not that elaborate. We'll often watch a movie, have a family soccer game, or go to a video arcade to just play together.

Wow, thank you, Jodie!

Something very unique and special about my wife is that she does a great job of listening to others, pursuing other people and letting them know that they're loved and cared for. She makes other people the hero of conversations.

Although she is not involved in the day-to-day rhythms of my work, she is very connected to my work's purpose. As a result, she supports me well and works to help Stewardship love people through finances in her own unique ways.

I have a special relationship with my wife, and I feel so appreciated by her—but that doesn't just happen. It bounces up in multiple instances. Last night, for example, we were sitting in bed and she just started telling me how appreciative she is of me. She told me how hard I work and how thankful she is that I provide for our family, and she's glad to be married to me. And that feels wonderful.

I want you to feel that way, too.

A lot of people tell me, "Oh man, I could never do this." But you can. As you saw from Jodie, I'm not perfect. I make mistakes. This whole pursuit of work-life harmony is a process. In each chapter, you have to provide those things for yourself, for your spouse, and for your family.

I hope you have someone as supportive in your life, that you're not trying to do it all on your own. There is value in having a supportive spouse; that's part of this process. Having someone on your team makes harmony come to life.

If you want to increase joy in your relationships, get on a mission together that is selfless and filled with serving other people. It is an absolute blast!

A QUICK WIN: AN ATTITUDE OF GRATITUDE

Take thirty minutes every week and look back at your calendar. Look at your tasks and appointments, look at the week that was, and take that time to pause and start being grateful.

I like to audibly pray and speak to God about the things I'm thankful for. Some people like to pick up a pen and write down things they're thankful for that week.

During that same time, pray, speak out loud, or write down the challenges you have coming up in the next week. What can you do differently this coming week, versus what you did last week, to help with those challenges?

Everybody stresses out about the challenges, so take time to just think and pray about them and determine one thing to do differently, to help with that stress.

Being thankful for things doesn't just come to us; it's not something you just absorb. The only way to be a grateful person is to practice gratitude. So even if you had the worst week ever last week, take the time to find one thing to be thankful for. As you practice taking that pause for gratitude, you'll become a more grateful person and that will give rest to some of the stress or negativity that may be present in your mind.

CONCLUSION

I had lunch yesterday with a friend who has made a ton of changes to his personal life, much of it coming from the conversations we have had around work–life harmony.

He used to struggle with achieving the ever-elusive work–life balance. He was doing his best, but he kept failing. At times, he gave up trying to have balance at all. And who could blame him? It hurts to fall off the balance beam over and over again. He resigned himself to the belief that his kids would grow up and their relationship would be whatever it was going to be; he was just going to drift and leave it all up to chance.

Until he asked me, "How do you get so much work done, but still make sure your family likes you?"

This question came from a place of fear. He wondered if he would be able to have a good relationship with his kids before they moved out of the house. And worse, he feared how disconnected he and his wife would be when that time came.

I told him about how I strive for harmony, not balance, and how that has helped me and my family live out our purpose even more—and that he deserved to have that harmony, too.

And now? He takes his kids out on a date once a week. He dates his wife, and they have a closer and better relationship than maybe ever before. Their family has more purpose, and, as a result, he has made adjustments to his daily rhythms so they have more time together in the evening.

In fact, their work–life harmony is in such a strong place that they started the foster-to-adopt process with a baby girl.

He didn't make wide, sweeping changes to his life and earn this progress in one week, one month, or even one year. It took a few years. But each year, things got progressively better.

Things are now *so* good for him that in our lunch conversation he was challenging me on rhythms that I needed to add to my life! Now, a few times a week I read the Bible out loud as we make our plates at dinnertime.

Work–life harmony has a compounding effect. It's important in my life, but it's completely changed his life—and the life of his wife, his boys, and their new foster sister. And as they continue to live in that harmony, that ripple effect will continue to be felt for generations.

LIVE YOUR PURPOSE, IN HARMONY

I believe I was put on this earth to love others.

I also believe that we can be amazing parents and spouses while also being amazing members of a team at work. When you have a purpose, and you invite your family and your work into that purpose, to work toward living out an ideal year, it will have a positive impact on every aspect of your life. You will be a more connected parent and spouse. You will be more intentional about your rest and evaluate how you're doing, so you're always trying to get better.

When you do that, your household is in a very healthy place—and it has the opportunity to make an impact on other households that aren't as healthy. Maybe you give financially to philanthropic endeavors. Maybe your household is a blessing to other households that are going through a tough time.

I pursue harmony because I believe it makes the world a better place. Because I believe it helps meet my mission of loving people well—at home, at work, and on the world as a whole.

I wrote this book to meet my purpose of loving them. In my heart and my wife's heart, we pray to ask God to use us to love people well through this wonderful, beautiful medium.

I hope you feel loved. I hope that my family's purpose was lived out here in this book. I hope you find your purpose, invite your family and your work into it, and continue pursuing work–life harmony.

When you are able to create work–life harmony, it transcends your life and begins to impact other people's lives as well. I taught the people I work with about the ideal year. I taught them about purpose. I coached them on all the things you've just read about in this book. And my employees see it. Work–life harmony is more than just me and my wife and our kids. Our work–life harmony has been seen and followed by others. And now it's impacting a ton of different households who are trying to do the things we do.

I want you to try what you've read in this book—and I want you to share it with other people, too. Don't keep it a secret. This is a journey, and other people are on it with you. The connectedness you seek with your work, your spouse, your family is something that everyone wants. You can talk about it with anyone, and you can share this book with anyone.

That will give you an opportunity to learn from them as they go through this journey, just as they will learn from you as you go through this journey.

If you want to find a way to grow as an individual, start teaching. I hope and pray that this book has an impact on thousands upon thousands of people, but there's no way it will have a bigger impact on anyone than it had on me by sharing it with you. When you become the teacher, the person who's being transparent and sharing their life, it multiplies your growth like it's on steroids. It takes it to a completely different level. My work–life harmony sounds even sweeter as a result of writing this book!

And the best way to start that growth...is to start. Do one thing you read about. Once it becomes a habit and you're doing well with it, come back to the book and start doing another thing. Share the things you've learned in this book with someone else, so you can be the teacher and take your growth to a whole other level.

Your goal is not to be Billy Joel or the Rolling Stones. Few people are. But with effort, with work, and with intention, by following the steps in this book, you can go from that second grader playing in the cringey school recital to the beautiful high school choir. You can have a work–life harmony that adds enjoyment to your life and gives you a great sense of pride.

YOU *CAN* DO THIS

Wow, that was a lot to read, huh? You may be feeling overwhelmed or wondering how you are going to put all of these steps into action.

First, you should know that I don't do all of these things every single day, all the time. Sometimes I forget something in my ideal year. There are things in my quarter or week that I don't get to 100 percent.

Life happens, and sometimes I forget something or intentionally skip something else. Sometimes my wife and I will look at each other and say, "We gotta do that *again?*" Then we'll enjoy the feeling of playing hooky as we purposely (and gleefully!) cross something off our calendar.

This is a compilation of all the things that I know work, and work well, when I'm doing them, so don't feel like it's a list of everything that you must get started on right now. If you're able to do 50 percent, or wow, 70 percent, you are doing great. Don't get discouraged.

You can do this.

After reading this book, it may sound like I'm some special person who has gifts outside of what most people have—but I'm just a normal guy, and there isn't really anything special about me. I didn't get the best grades in school or go to

Harvard. I grew up on a farm kicking cow patties for fun. If I can do it, you can too. *Anybody* can follow these steps. Again, you can do this.

YOU—AND YOUR LOVED ONES—*DESERVE* HARMONY

Not only can you do this, but you *deserve* to do it. You deserve harmony.

You were created to contribute, and that contribution matters. You deserve to have enjoyment in that contribution, and appreciation at home and at work. You deserve to have harmony and all the joy that comes with it.

Lastly, the people around you deserve it, too—so they need you to do this. The more harmony you have together, the more they are connected to the *why* of the things happening in your lives, and the better they can understand the expectations you set forth—the greater contributors *they* are going to become, too.

Work-life harmony impacts your life, but it also sets an example of what that looks like for your children. Now you're leaving a legacy and creating an opportunity for your grandkids to experience amazing work-life harmony—and their grandkids, and so on down the line. Generations of people you will never meet will be able to have this amazing benefit of a harmonious life because you put in the work.

Because you got all the members of your band on the same page (the ideal year calendar), kept everyone on the right tempo (rhythms, efficiencies, rest, and evaluations), and presented the song in the proper key (the purpose), this song is being played together by all the people who matter most. And it's beautiful!

Someday, when they may have kids of their own, you'll hear your kids sing the same type of song that you started singing to them when they were younger. You'll recognize the melody, your harmony will continue, and it will bring you a smile filled with a wonderful joy and peace.

RESOURCES

Here are all the resources referenced throughout this book, all in one convenient place!

QUICK WINS

- One Kid Up: Create a rhythm of staying up with one of your kids one night a week.
- Say Thank You: Tell one of your loved ones thank you for the success that you've had and how, specifically, they've played a part in your success.
- The Most Wonderful Time of the Year: Think of someone in need and, with your family, secretly drop off whatever will serve that person's need.
- Time to Come Home: Each day, before you leave for work, let your family know what time you plan to come

home—and be sure to let them know if those plans change.

- Your Go-To Vacation: Come up with go-to places to rest or celebrate with your family, including a favorite restaurant, staycation plans, and a preplanned destination for a minivacation.
- Give 'Em a Rest: Support your spouse or partner by providing intentional time for them to rest in whatever way is most meaningful to them.
- Let Them Evaluate You: Ask your spouse/partner and/or kids to evaluate you by asking them how you're doing as a spouse or parent, what you should keep doing, and what you may want to do differently.
- An Attitude of Gratitude: Take thirty minutes each week to practice gratitude for the previous week and prepare for any potential challenges in the upcoming week.

RESOURCES FROM OTHER PEOPLE

Amy Porterfield's podcast episode on batch-work: https://www.amyporterfield.com/2017/10/182-how-to-mega-batch-your-content

Michael Hyatt's Full Focus Planner: https://fullfocusplanner.com

The Family Teams Calendar by Jefferson Bethke: https://shop.familyteams.com/products/family-plan-calendar

The Purpose Driven Life by Rick Warren

Clockwork by Mike Michalowicz

RESOURCES FROM GRANT

The Problem Isn't Their Paycheck: How to Attract Top Talent and Build a Thriving Company Culture by Grant Botma

Grant's Ideal Year Calendar video:
https://www.grantbotma.com/calendar

Follow Grant on social media:

🐦 @GrantBotma

📷 @GrantBotma

ACKNOWLEDGMENTS

Most people acknowledge their spouse and their kids in their books. And, of course, in a book about work–life harmony, I gotta do the same! But I want to communicate this acknowledgment with genuine authenticity. These aren't just words; this isn't just a token acknowledgment.

I genuinely need to acknowledge my wife, Jodie, for walking through this journey of work–life harmony since day one of our marriage. I am not the perfect spouse, I am not the perfect parent, but her grace, her love, and her support have allowed this work–life harmony journey to move in a positive direction, year after year. Because of her, we have a special relationship, a special family, and an extremely special life. Without her, not only does this book not happen, but that special life doesn't happen either.

I also need, and genuinely want, to acknowledge my children for having grace for me in learning how to be a parent and learning how to have work–life harmony. For loving and supporting the purpose of our family, of my life, to love others, but also for learning to take ownership of and enjoying watching the purpose of Stewardship come to life in loving people through finances. Each of my children is unique and special in their own way, but together we are unified around a purpose that creates a special family.

The family member, and friend, who has given me the most motivation to pursue work–life harmony is my brother-in-law, Daniel Stratman. I know your life is not exactly how you would want it. I too wish you were without disability and able to live a "normal" life. But, as I have told you before, I "consider it pure joy" and choose to praise God for your injury. Your life has had a profound impact on mine in more ways than I could count. One of those ways is how you have provided a motivation to find work–life harmony, find it quickly, and work to get better at it each day. I would not be the husband, father, and business owner I am today if it wasn't for you. Thank you!

I also want to acknowledge my business partners, Brandon Ream and Jake Norton, for supporting me in writing this book as we run our business and do our best to love our community through finances. Thank you, also, to the entire Stewardship team for trusting me. Most employees don't allow their employer to speak into their personal lives, and you guys do that. You allow me to share with you where I've made mistakes and where I've had success in my personal life so that you too can grow. That means that you trust me, and I don't take that trust lightly. Thank you.

Professionally speaking, I would also like to acknowledge several people who have influenced this journey and provided resources and information about work–life harmony to help me learn and grow: people like Rick Warren, Andy Stanley, Amy Porterfield, and Michael Hyatt.

I also want to acknowledge my home church, Sun Valley Community Church, and my pastors and friends, Chad Moore and Robert Watson, as they have not only led a church community that allows me and my family to serve together, but have been used by the Lord to speak into my life and challenge me to keep pursuing a more harmonious life.

ABOUT THE AUTHOR

GRANT BOTMA is a husband, dad, author, keynote speaker, entrepreneur, and founder of Stewardship, where he is a licensed investment advisor, loan originator, mortgage broker, and insurance agent. Stewardship was voted an Inc. 5000 Fastest-Growing Company in America, and Botma was named a top entrepreneur before he reached the age of thirty-five. Most importantly, he makes an impact in his community by loving people through finances.

Botma is also the author of the bestselling book *The Problem Isn't Their Paycheck: How to Attract Top Talent and Build a Thriving Company Culture.* He is an avid sports enthusiast and a big Cubs fan.

An Arizona native, Botma grew up on a dairy farm in Buckeye, Arizona. He attended Arizona Christian University, where he majored in business administration and Christian ministries. He and his wife, Jodie, currently live in Gilbert, Arizona, with their three children, Cambria, Parker, and Ellenie, where they attend Sun Valley Community Church. Together, they pursue their family's purpose of loving others.

If you're interested in connecting with Grant personally, you can follow him on Twitter or Instagram, @GrantBotma.

Made in United States
Orlando, FL
19 May 2023

33267719R00140